HIDDEN LIVES

The Archaeology of Slave Life at
Thomas Jefferson's Poplar Forest

HIDDEN LIVES

The Archaeology of Slave Life at Thomas Jefferson's Poplar Forest

Barbara J. Heath

UNIVERSITY PRESS OF VIRGINIA

Charlottesville and London

THE UNIVERSITY PRESS OF VIRGINIA

© 1999 by the Rector and Visitors of the University of Virginia

All rights reserved

Printed in the United States of America

First published 1999

⊗ The paper used in this publication meets the minimum requirements of the American National Standard for Information Sciences—Permanence of Paper for Printed Library Materials, ANSI Z39.48-1984.

Library of Congress Cataloging-in-Publication Data

Heath, Barbara J., 1960–

    Hidden lives : the archaeology of slave life at Thomas Jefferson's Poplar Forest / Barbara J. Heath.

      p. cm.

    Includes bibliographical references and index.

    ISBN 0-8139-1867-7 (paper : alk. paper)

    1. Poplar Forest (Va.)—History. 2. Slaves—Virginia—Bedford County—History—18th century. 3. Bedford County (Va.)—Antiquities. 4. Excavations (Archaelogy)—Virginia—Bedford County. 5. Plantation life—Virginia—Bedford County—History—18th century. 6. Jefferson, Thomas, 1743–1826—Homes and haunts—Virginia—Bedford County. I. Title.

E332.74.H43   1999

975.5'675—dc21

98-45247

CIP

Contents

Illustrations

Acknowledgments

Archaeology is a team undertaking. Led by Poplar Forest's professional archaeologists, the team that excavated, analyzed, researched, and funded the project described in this book consisted of teachers and college students, librarians and retired chemists, philanthropists and anthropologists.

The financial support of the Henry Luce Foundation, which provided funding for all phases of this project, is gratefully acknowledged. Thanks also go to the numerous corporate, government, and individual sponsors of the Corporation for Jefferson's Poplar Forest who have provided long-term financial support for the Corporation's archaeological programs, to the Poplar Forest Board of Directors, and to Executive Director Lynn Beebe.

The following staff, interns, and volunteers have contributed greatly to the project: Keith Adams, Rene Andrews, Susan Trevarthen Andrews, Marca Wesen Bondurant, George Bonnett, Alasdair Brooks, Randi Campbell, Hannah Canel, Donald Cushman, Chip Dull, Pat Everett, Lisa Fischer, Amanda Fitch, Jean Fulton, Ruth Glass, Dr. Nancy Lane, Fursey McCormack, Amber Bennett Moncure, Martha Moore, Jim Neese, Liz Paull, Elaine Davis Phillips, Rick Potter, Daniel Richardson, Dot O'Connor, Brent Sonnemaker, Ben Skove, and Michael Strutt.

I am grateful to the participants in the 1993-96 University of Virginia–Poplar Forest archaeological field schools and to the teachers who took part in the annual seminar "Digging, Learning, and Teaching:

Archaeology for Teachers at Poplar Forest." For their hard work and good spirits in the hot Virginia sun, I thank them.

My thanks are also extended to a number of colleagues who assisted in various aspects of the conservation, analysis, and interpretation of the site: Linda Baumgarten, Edward Chappell, Martin Dranoff, Jay Gaynor, David Harvey, Michael Hartley, John Larson, Ann Lucas, Curt Moyer, Leslie Raymer, Bradford Rauschenberg, Kurt Russ, and Kate Singley.

I also thank the staff of the Special Collections Library at Duke University for their assistance with the John Hook papers, staff members at the Special Collections Department, University of Virginia Library, and the staff of the Rosenbach Museum and Library for providing access to Jefferson materials in their collections.

Finally, I would like to thank Kathy Osmus and my colleagues at Poplar Forest for their careful reading of the draft of this manuscript. Their comments have helped me to write with greater clarity and focus. Any errors or omissions are, of course, my responsibility.

HIDDEN LIVES

The Archaeology of Slave Life at Thomas Jefferson's Poplar Forest

1 Introduction

A STAND OF TULIP POPLARS, battered by storms and brittle with age, rises above an old brick house in the rolling hills of central Virginia. These ancient giants once formed part of a wood that gave this land its name, Poplar Forest, sometime before 1745. Here Thomas Jefferson, weary from years of public service, found peaceful retirement. In 1806, during his second term as president of the United States, he began construction of a retreat house some ninety miles southwest of his Monticello plantation. He set it beneath the poplars' canopy and found within it "the solitude of a hermit" (fig. 1).[1]

FIG. 1. Poplar trees north of Jefferson's octagonal house at Poplar Forest

FIG. 2. Aerial photograph of Poplar Forest showing Jefferson's retreat house in the center left with the quarter site in the lower right behind houses

Just to the northeast, a second grove of gnarled poplars, roots set deep in the red piedmont clay, guards the edge of a grass-covered hillside. It is likely that here, amid the poplars and the fields and meadows that once surrounded them, a younger Thomas Jefferson sought refuge for himself and his family during a summer late in the course of the American Revolution. Most probably, he spent that season in the house of his plantation overseer, a practice he would continue during future visits until he decided to build a home for himself (fig. 2).[2]

Others knew this landscape well, for in the closing years of the 1700s and the opening decade of the new century, a group of enslaved men, women, and children lived in log buildings perched on the hillside. Some spent their days toiling in the plantation's fields. Others learned a craft, balancing hours in the fields with time at home or in the shops. In the quiet of the evenings and the respite from assigned work that Sundays provided, they experienced the joys and sorrows of private life.

In 1993 archaeologists began to uncover the remnants of buildings and yards once occupied by these African Americans (fig. 3). Soil stains, when carefully mapped and excavated, revealed the presence of storage pits, burned tree roots, and postholes. Fragments of ceramics, glass, and iron, scattered through the soils of the site, mended to become bottles, plates, and cooking pots. Over three seasons in the field and in the laboratory, the story of this site, the quarter site, gradually came together.

This book tells that story as part of the larger narrative of the Poplar Forest slave community. Woven from terse lists of births and deaths, postscripts to letters, sherds of pottery, and fragments of bone, the tale is, like the evidence that informs it, incomplete. Human experience cannot be recovered from the detritus of everyday life. Yet even a partial story opens a fascinating window into the past, creating new understandings and raising fresh questions. This study has done both.

FIG. 3. Excavations at the quarter in 1993. Note the partially excavated root cellar in the right background.

Finding "The Old Plantation"

Poplar Forest, once owned by Thomas Jefferson, is now a private museum dedicated to discovering, preserving, and restoring evidence of Jefferson's life, the house he built, the landscape he designed, and the plantation he managed. Since 1989, archaeologists have been exploring the grounds, looking for clues about the residents and landscape of the eighteenth- and early nineteenth-century plantation.

In the spring of 1993, archaeologists began to dig a series of small test holes along the hillside east of the poplar grove. The exercise was straightforward: before planting some trees, the museum staff needed to examine the area to ensure that nothing of historic importance was destroyed.

Archaeologists soon discovered that part of this hillside had once been farmed. Repeated plowing had mixed soil layers, creating a single, homogeneous plow zone of about six to eight inches in depth. Excavators quickly began to uncover small fragments of English ceramics common in the late eighteenth and early nineteenth centuries, hand-forged, or wrought, nails, and other artifacts typical of that period scattered throughout the plow zone.

The excavation of one test hole led to the discovery of something more substantial alongside these seemingly random finds. A deposit of dark, charcoal-enriched soil extended down into the ground. Excavators expanded the test hole to expose a ten-foot area. Within its boundaries the deposit of disturbed earth formed a dark brown stain against the red piedmont clay. As ceramics, bottle glass, buttons, beads, buckles, animal bones, nails, burned daub, and discarded tools began to emerge from distinct layers within the deepening pit, it became obvious that the archaeologists had found a small cellar associated with a house that stood here during Jefferson's ownership of the property (fig. 4). Finding evidence of a house raised the question: who had lived here?

A series of maps dating from the late eighteenth century to about

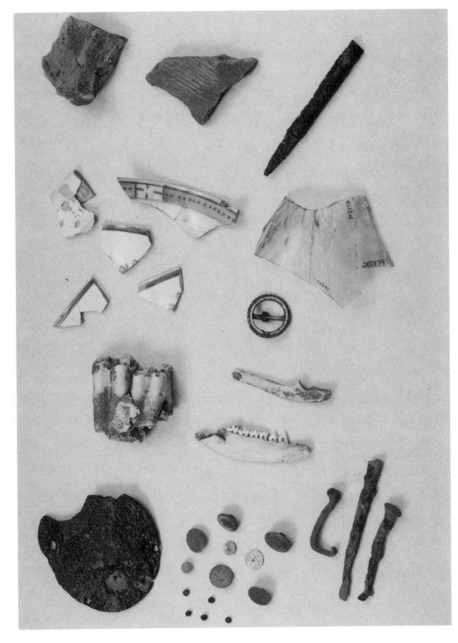

FIG. 4. Artifacts recovered from root cellar in structure 1. *Top left to bottom right*: daub, half-round file, creamware, pearlware, mold-blown bottle, buckle, cow jaw fragment, opossum ulna and jaw, padlock faceplate, buttons, beads, wrought nails.

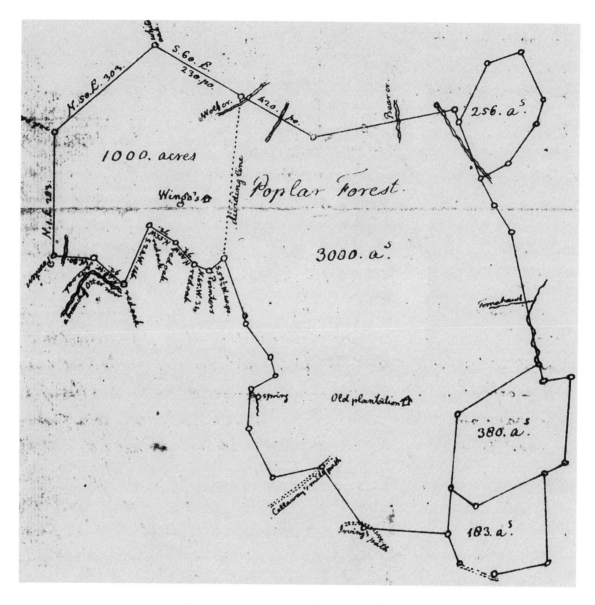

FIG. 5. Plat of Poplar Forest, 1790, showing the location of the "Old plantation"

1801 shows the location of at least one building situated south and west of the site. One mapmaker had labeled this structure "Old plantation," suggesting that by 1790 the area had been inhabited for several years (fig. 5). Other surveyors portrayed a building labeled either "Overseer's house" or "Mansion House" in the same location. While today the term *mansion* describes a grand estate occupied by people of wealth, in 1800 it was only rarely used in that way. Most often, it simply meant "a dwelling house" or referred to the house of the landowner, whether

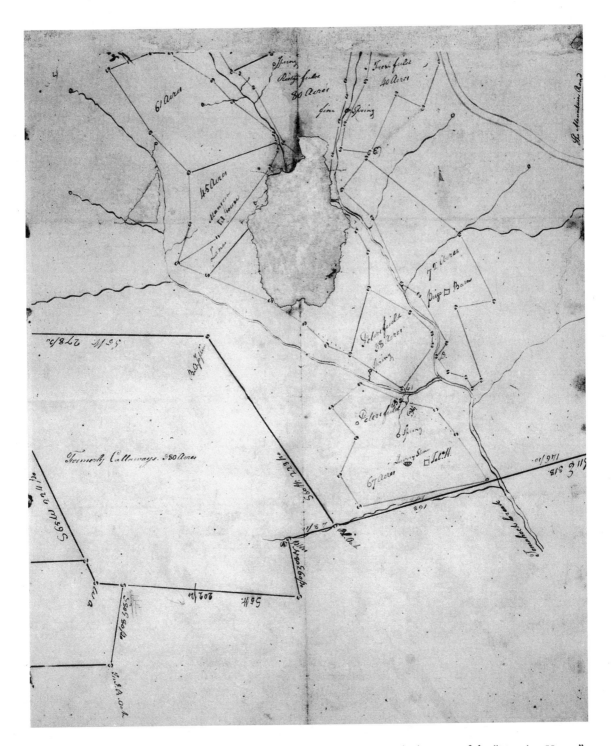

FIG. 6. Plat of Poplar Forest, c. 1800, showing the location of the "Mansion House"

grand or modest. It is probable that this was the dwelling of the over-seer; however, there may have been two adjoining houses at the center of this plantation complex.[1] Despite the questions these maps raise, they clearly show that this area was the hub of the Poplar Forest plantation decades before Jefferson built his retreat house.

When placed on these early maps, the archaeological site appears to lie between the mansion house and a narrow strip of land called the "Lane" (fig. 6). No buildings are depicted on any of the maps in this location. Clearly, the maps were incomplete. Among other omissions, they left out the slave quarters.

While much of the story of the enslaved community at Poplar Forest lay sealed within the soils of the site, an equally important part was buried in archival sources and published accounts of Jefferson's life. Before exploring the archaeological aspects of the site, it is important to understand the recorded history of the property.

3

The Enslaved Community
at Poplar Forest

Early History

IT IS NOT KNOWN when the first enslaved men and women arrived at Poplar Forest, for records from the early history of the property are scarce and lacking in detail. While it is possible that people lived and worked on the plantation before the 1760s, the first known reference to slaves appears in 1766. In that year the Bedford County Court ordered that hands belonging to John Wayles assist in roadwork.[1] It is with Wayles, then, that the story of slavery at Poplar Forest unfolds on a spring day in 1773.

On May 28 of that year, John Wayles, father, businessman, and planter, died at his home in Charles City County at the age of fifty-eight. His death profoundly affected the lives of his family and those of the enslaved men and women living and working in communities scattered across his vast holdings in central Virginia.

For son-in-law Thomas Jefferson, Wayles's passing initially seemed a guarantee of his own future wealth. On behalf of his wife Martha, Jefferson inherited 135 slaves and over 11,000 acres of land from the Wayles estate. Along with land in Amelia, Cumberland, and Goochland counties, the Jeffersons took possession of two plantations in Bedford: Poplar Forest and Judith's Creek, also known as Dunlora. In eighteenth-century Virginia land and the labor force to work it productively were the keys to success. Jefferson planned to use the inherited lands as sources of revenue to support his family at his home plantation, Monticello, in Albemarle County.[2]

John Wayles died deeply in debt, however, and along with the benefits of inheritance came the burden of repayment. Jefferson sold much of his newly acquired land on the eve of the American Revolution in an effort to meet his share of Wayles's financial obligations. Yet these sales failed to settle the debt. Some land was purchased from Jefferson on personal bonds that Wayles's creditors refused to honor. Some was paid for with currency that lost its value during the war.[3] By war's end Jefferson's debt had grown. In spite of his efforts at repayment, it continued to grow during the following decades. By the 1790s Jefferson had sold nearly all of his inherited lands. He retained only Poplar Forest.

While Wayles's death had a long-term effect on his son-in-law's financial life, it had a much more immediate and direct effect on the lives of his bondsmen and women. By splitting the estate between family members, Wayles's will irrevocably divided enslaved families and neighbors from each other and from their homes.

In January 1774 Thomas Jefferson listed the men and women that he had acquired from his father-in-law's estate (fig. 7). He recorded a single family living at Poplar Forest, noting that Guinea Will and his twenty-six-year-old wife Betty worked as "laborers in the ground." Six-year-old Hall, their eldest child, probably spent his days looking after his sisters Dilcey and Suckey, aged four and two. Twenty-year-old Billy Boy, the only other enslaved person listed for the property, was a blacksmith. Most likely, he lived and worked alongside Joshua Brock, a hired smith who operated a shop at Poplar Forest during the 1770s. Five other men and women, John, Davy, Mary, Doll, and Charles, lived at Wingos, a one-thousand-acre farm located in the northwest corner of the larger Poplar Forest tract. Four of the five were aged twenty or younger, and Jefferson listed all but Mary as laborers.[4]

FIG. 7. Slave census, January 1774, from Jefferson's Farm Book

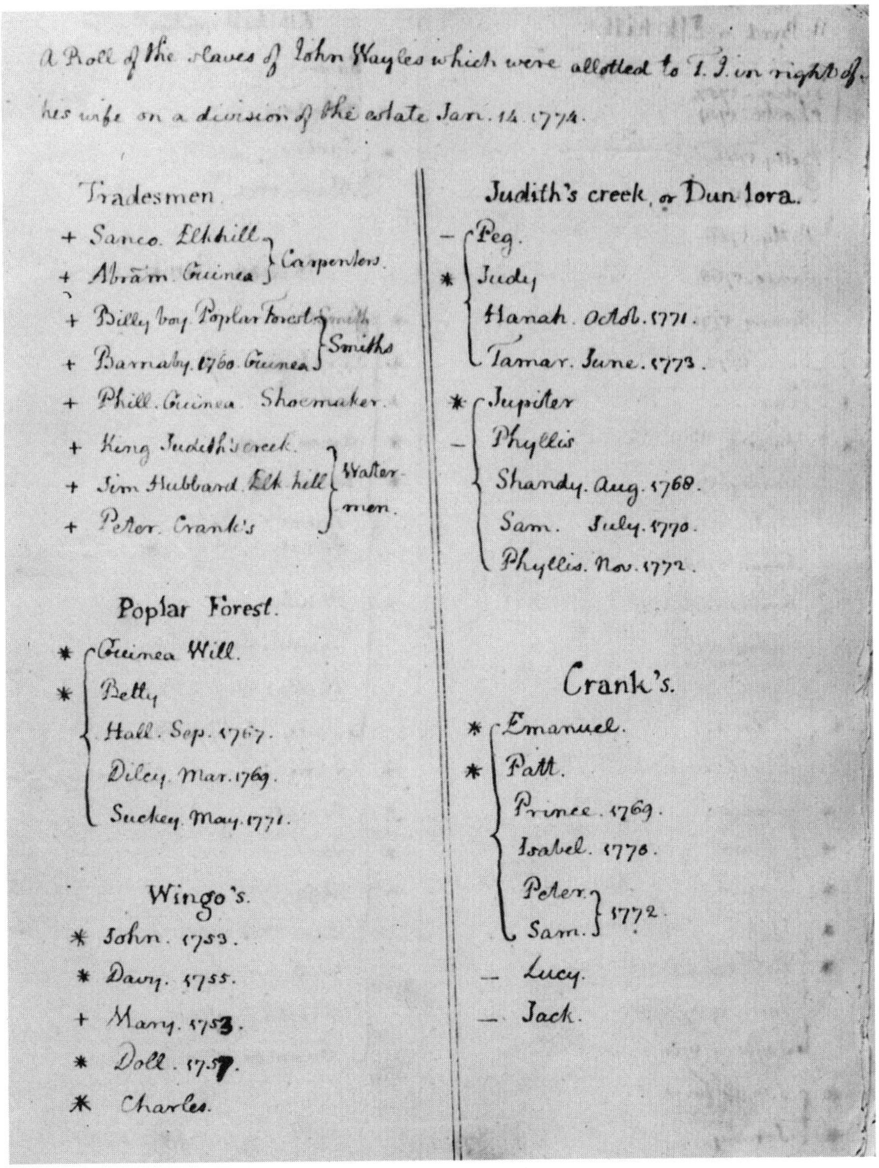

A Roll of the slaves of John Wayles which were allotted to T. J. in right of his wife on a division of the estate Jan. 14. 1774.

Tradesmen.
+ Sanco. Elkhill
+ Abram. Guinea } Carpenters.
+ Billy boy. Poplar Forest Smith
+ Barnaby. 1760. Guinea } Smiths
+ Phill. Guinea. Shoemaker.
+ King. Judith's creek
+ Jim Hubbard. Elk hill } Watermen.
+ Peter. Crank's

Poplar Forest.
* Guinea Will.
* Betty
   Hall. Sep. 1767.
   Dilcy. Mar. 1769.
   Suckey. May. 1771.

Wingo's.
* John. 1753.
* Davy. 1755.
+ Mary. 1753.
* Doll. 1757.
* Charles.

Judith's creek, or Dunlora.
— Peg.
* Judy
   Hanah. Octob. 1771.
   Tamar. June. 1773.
* Jupiter
— Phyllis
   Shandy. Aug. 1768.
   Sam. July. 1770.
   Phyllis. Nov. 1772.

Crank's.
* Emanuel.
* Patt.
   Prince. 1769.
   Isabel. 1770.
   Peter
   Sam. } 1772.
— Lucy.
— Jack.

Later that year, the combined population of Poplar Forest and Wingos nearly tripled as Jefferson organized his newly acquired workforce. Enslaved men and women from Monticello, Elk Hill, Indian Camp, and Judith's Creek moved to Poplar Forest, so that by 1783 thirty-five people lived there. This was the third home for some, like Dinah and Solomon, in less than ten years.[5] With the ongoing sales of land, men and women continued to move between plantations.

During the early 1790s Jefferson gathered forty slaves from his properties and sold them in Bedford County. He gave an additional thirty-five bondspeople—twenty-seven from the Poplar Forest estate—to his daughter Martha upon the occasion of her marriage. By mid-decade, a degree of stability began to emerge. The community of interrelated families that had begun to take root earlier was allowed to grow, with only periodic disruptions.[6]

To Be a Slave

By the time of Jefferson's inheritance, slavery had been codified in Virginia law for over a century. To be a slave meant to be at once human and chattel, property that could be bought or sold on an owner's whim. Enslaved mothers passed this status on to their children, guaranteeing a self-perpetuating system.

Within this rigid structure, individuals struggled to maintain some control over their lives. The degree to which they succeeded was often dictated by the external circumstances of their bondage: when they lived, where they lived, and who their owner was. Yet the choices that they made were also significant in determining the direction of their lives.

The study of the enslaved community at Poplar Forest underlines the importance of external change. While future archaeological investigations will continue to clarify the pace and nature of this change, it is clear that historical events, like the American Revolution and the War of 1812, and personal events, like the death of John Wayles or Jefferson's decision to build a home on the property, significantly affected the lives of Poplar Forest residents. Yet the stories of individuals like Nace who was accused of stealing vegetables from the garden and selling them at market, Phil Hubbard who ran away to protest mistreatment, or Maria who learned to be "a capital spinner" reveal the ways in which personal choices also shaped individual lives.[7]

Family Life

By the 1790s members of seven enslaved families lived at Poplar Forest (fig. 8). At the time of Jefferson's death in 1826, as many as four generations of a single family lived on the property.

Although slave marriages were not legally recognized, Jefferson respected and sanctioned common-law unions. He encouraged young people to choose a mate from within the Poplar Forest community, thereby ensuring that spouses would not be separated by sales over which he had no control and that future children born within the marriage might remain as workers on his plantations. His desire to protect family life stemmed in part from a wish to see "his people" happy, yet he clearly understood the advantages of a stable workforce. In an 1819 letter to overseer Joel Yancey, Jefferson explored the economic benefits of family life by noting that "a child raised every 2. Years is of more profit than the crop of the best laboring man. In this, as in all other cases, providence has made our interest and our duties coincide perfectly."[8]

While Jefferson made an effort to keep families intact, he treated teenagers as he would unmarried adults, sending some away from home to work at Monticello. He sold those who chose to resist the conditions of slavery actively through violence or through flight, thereby severing family ties.[9]

Jefferson rewarded women who chose a spouse from among the eligible Poplar Forest men with a pot, a bed, and when possible, a house. While some young people followed their owner's wishes, others chose husbands and wives living on neighboring plantations or in town. This meant that spouses often continued to live apart at their places of servitude, and children stayed with their mothers. According to the census lists Jefferson kept between 1774 and 1811, women headed several households at Poplar Forest, suggesting that it was not always easy, or desirable, to find a spouse within the plantation community.[10]

Negroes in Bedford
July 1805.
Jame Hubbard
Cate. ab. 1749.
Armistead. 71.
Nace. 73.
Sarah. 88. aug.
Nancy 91. Sep. Oct. 08
Rachael. Oct. 73.
  Burrel. 94. d 1808
  Cate. 97. aug.
  Joe. 1801.
  Lania. 1805

Maria. 76.
  Nace 96. aug.
  Nisy. 99.
  Johnny 1804. Sep.

Eve. 79.
  Sanco. 97. Mar.

Will. smith.
Abbey
  Jesse. 72. Nov.
  Dick. 81. Oct.
  Fanny 88. aug.
  Edy. 92. Apr.
  Armistead. 94. (Manuel)
  Amy. 97. Jan.

Sal. 77. Nov.
  Isbel. June 95 d 07
  Milley 97. Mar.
  Betty 1801. Jan.
  Abbey. 1804. Nov.

Flora. 83.
  Gawen. 1804. July

Hanah. (Cate's) 70. Jan
  Lucinda. 91. June
  Reuben. 93.
  Solomon. 94.
  Salley 98.
  Billy 99.
  Janney 1805. aug.

Bess. (Guinea Will's)
  Hal. (smith) 67. Sep.
  Caesar. 74. Sep.

Suck (Bess's) 71. May
  Cate 88. Mar.
  Daniel 90. Sep.
  Stephen. 94.
  Philip. 96.
  Ambrose 99.
  Prince. 1804.

Hercules. ab 1733. d. 180
Bet.
  Austin. 75. aug.
  Gawen. 78. aug.
  Cate 88. Mar. 8
  Mary. 92. Jan.
  Hercules. 94. Nov. 20.
  Jupiter. 1800. Mar. d. 1809.

Dick. 67.
Dinah. 66.
  John 85. Nov.
  Aggey. 89. Mar.
  Moses. 92. Jan.
  Evans. 94.
  Hanah. 96. aug.
  Lucy 99.
  Jamey. 1802.

Judy (old)

Nanny (Phill's) 78. July.
  Maria. 98. Feb. 24.
  Phill. 1801. aug.
  Polley 1804. July. d 1807.

Lucy. (Phill's) 83. July
  Robin. 1805.

It is difficult to ascertain when individuals married, since it is unlikely that a register of such events was kept. However, Jefferson did record the birth dates of all children born on the property, so it is possible to track the growth of families. Young women typically bore their first child between the ages of eighteen and twenty. The first two generations of Poplar Forest women averaged eight children each. It is harder to trace the family histories of men, since many may have chosen spouses living off the plantation, and records of their children may not survive. On average, men who chose wives from among the women at Poplar Forest fathered their first child at age twenty-five. Nearly all men and women who lost a spouse remarried.[11]

Relatively stable kinship networks provided a system of social support within the plantation. Young people learned valuable lessons from their parents, grandparents, uncles, and aunts. When nuclear families were disrupted by death, sale, or the movement of a parent or child to another of Jefferson's farms, members of the extended family stepped in to fill needed roles within the household. Eventually, these kin networks grew beyond Bedford, extending across central Virginia to Jefferson's Albemarle County holdings.

Life and Work

For men and women living in bondage at Poplar Forest, as throughout the South, life and labor became synonymous at an early age. The workday lasted from sunup to sundown, the workweek from Monday through Saturday. Only evenings and Sundays were left free for toil at home, visits to Lynchburg and New London, or socializing with family and neighbors. Field hands and artisans transformed themselves into storytellers and musicians as the sun set, sharing their experiences through tales and songs. Slaves enjoyed a brief respite at Christmas, when some were allowed to travel between Poplar Forest and Monticello to visit relatives and friends.[12]

Jefferson directed that children ten years old and younger should serve as nurses to their siblings. Children and teenagers also helped their parents in the fields, performing less strenuous jobs like weeding, planting seeds, and gathering wheat.

Beginning in the 1790s, Jefferson sent boys between the ages of ten and sixteen to his Albemarle headquarters, where they learned to make nails in the plantation nailery. Among those who went to live and work at Monticello were John, Davy, and brothers Phil and Jame Hubbard. Others stayed behind and labored in the fields.

In 1811 Jefferson assigned four twelve- and thirteen-year-old girls to spin at the homes of some of the older women living on the plantation. Lucy and Sally worked with Bess and Abby, while Nisy and Maria learned from Cate, the grandmother of one and great-aunt of the other. The following winter Maria and Sally journeyed to Monticello to learn to weave and spin on the spinning jenny. Jefferson praised Maria's progress, while at the same time lamenting that he had never seen "so hopeless a subject" as Sally. Upon the latter's return home, Jefferson instructed that his overseer choose a more promising girl from those working "in the ground" to replace her. Two years later Poplar Forest had its own spinning house, and girls no longer had to travel to Monticello to learn their craft.[13]

At age sixteen young men and women began their long-term roles within the plantation labor force. Some learned a trade and worked as carpenters, smiths, weavers, or coopers as adults. Others "went into the ground," tending the plantation's crops and livestock until old age or infirmity forced them into another role. Older slaves continued to work as long as they were able. In 1811 sixty-four-year-old Bess divided her time between the dairy and her own home, where she spun wool for cloth. Will, a blacksmith, was still active in the shop at age fifty-eight. "Old Judy," who died at age eighty-two in 1810, probably spent her last years attending to children at home while their parents worked elsewhere on the plantation.[14]

A few men, such as Jame Hubbard and Nace, were chosen as foremen, or headmen, for the field crews.[15] Tied to the community by bonds of blood and marriage yet charged with authority and privileged in ways that other slaves were not, these men spent their lives balanced between two worlds (fig. 9).

FIG. 9. Plat of Poplar Forest, c. 1800, showing the location of slave headman Jame Hubbard's house

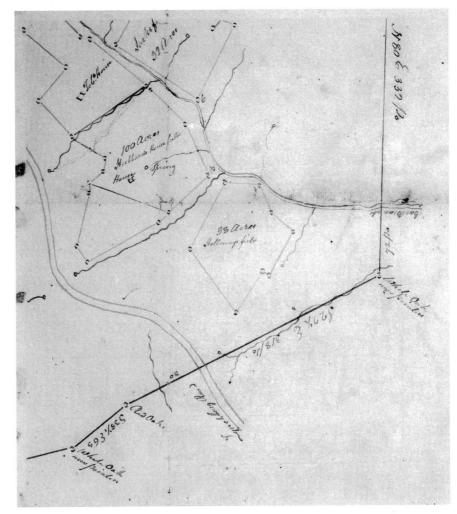

Health and Healing

Slaves endured a variety of infirmities during their lives. Letters, accounts, and census data indicate that people suffered from a range of maladies and disabilities, while fragments of glass pharmaceutical bottles found at the site mark the consumption of remedies prescribed by white doctors. Contagious diseases such as measles, dysentery, and whooping cough spread easily in an age when houses were close together and sanitation was poor. Children were particularly susceptible to illness, and Jefferson encouraged his overseers to allow women to tend their sick children without interference. Adults suffered from complications of childbirth, work-related injuries or accidents, and a host of maladies.[16]

To treat certain illnesses, Jefferson engaged a neighboring doctor who used a course of prescription drugs, bleeding, and blistering to effect a cure. In most cases Jefferson felt "a dose of salts," "a lighter diet," and "kind attention" to be preferable to treatments by medical professionals.[17] He advised his overseer to keep sugar, molasses, and salts "in the house for the sick," instructions that suggest the presence of a plantation hospital.

Slaves maintained healing traditions of their own, combining elements of West African spiritual beliefs with herbal remedies. Some remedies were known and shared within the quarter, while for more serious illnesses people consulted "Negro doctors."

On one occasion at Poplar Forest, the ministrations of a "Negro doctor" were unsuccessful (fig. 10). Several slaves accused Hercules, who had obtained medicine from him, of poisoning the sick.[18] The charges ultimately could not be proved. It was probably quite common for enslaved men and women to rely on folk healers from within the African-American community, turning only to the overseer when such methods failed.[19]

By the late eighteenth century, smokers primarily consumed tobacco

Fig. 10. Letter from overseer Joel Yancey to Thomas Jefferson, discussing use of "Negro doctor"

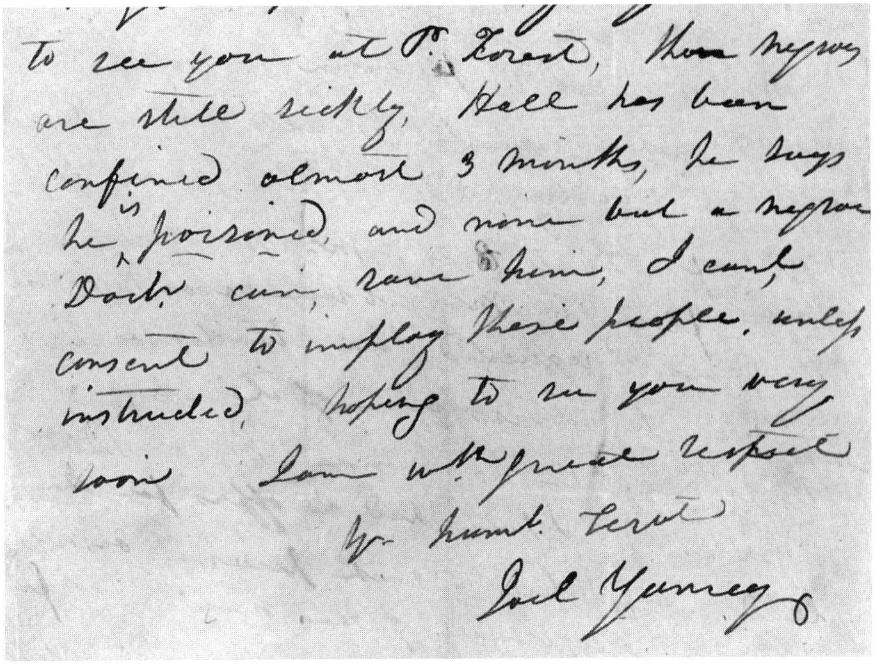
to see you at P. Forest, those negroes
are still sickly, Hall has been
confined almost 3 months, he says
he is poisoned, and none but a negro
Doct. can save him, I cant
consent to imploy these people, unless
instructed, hoping to see you very
soon I am with great respect
yr. humb. servt
Joel Yancey

as a luxury item, yet its use was rooted in the belief that tobacco smoke contained healing properties. Other plants also may have been smoked to relieve the symptoms of disease. An assortment of mass-produced English and Virginian pipes has been found at the site, in addition to an assemblage of homemade pipes made of stone (fig. 11). In the practice of their art, healers also used herbs in preparing teas and poultices. Archaeologists recovered many carbonized plant remains from the site, including pokeweed, goosefoot, smartweed, and bedstraw, that may have been used in folk medicine.[20]

Cycles of Work

Planters on older properties throughout Virginia abandoned tobacco cultivation during the closing decades of the eighteenth century as the long-term effects of soil exhaustion and erosion took their toll. Because Poplar Forest had been farmed for a relatively short period of time, the

FIG. 11. Fragments of tobacco pipes found at the quarter

property combined fresher fields with an abundance of woodland that could be cleared for cultivation. As a result, Jefferson continued to rely upon tobacco grown at Poplar Forest as a cash crop even after he ceased to grow it elsewhere. After the introduction of wheat in the 1790s, it became the other principal crop grown for sale.

On the plantation the pace of life revolved around an agricultural schedule set by the need to bring these two crops to market. Enslaved workers also raised many of the basic foods that Jefferson allotted to them and to the overseers' families after harvest. They grew provisions and cared for the cows, horses, oxen, pigs, and sheep that lived on the plantation and in turn used these animals for meat, wool, hides, or labor.[21]

Records of the Poplar Forest crop indicate that slaves planted and tended between 80,000 and 300,000 hillocks of tobacco each year (fig. 12).[22] Health and age permitting, everyone worked at least part-time in the fields and storehouses of the plantation. Field gangs consisted of an even mix of able-bodied men and women.

During the winter months hands spent much of their time clearing trees and brush from untilled land and plowing established fields. Wood was split into rails for new fences or for repairing existing ones. When necessary, men and women also built roads at this time of year. Late in the season, some slaves planted hemp for cloth and clover and grasses for fodder. Others carted and spread manure over fields to renew the soil.[23]

In the early spring planting continued. Seedbeds, placed beside creeks to take advantage of the fertile soils deposited by seasonal flooding, were tilled and sowed with tiny tobacco seeds. Slaves prepared tobacco fields by hoeing or plowing the ground, then forming hillocks about three-and-one-half feet apart into which the young plants would eventually be set (see fig. 12).

During the weeks that followed planting, slaves weeded the tobacco beds. They sowed corn, oats, potatoes, and pumpkins and attended to the birth of calves and lambs. Sheep were shorn of their winter wool. Milk cows, pastured for part of the year at Bear Creek, were driven to Tomahawk during the butter-making season. Stored in the dairy, butter was later carried to Monticello in the cool days of late fall.[24]

Transplanting young tobacco plants, a time-consuming and unpleasant task, occurred between mid-May and early June. To protect delicate roots, adults and children worked in the rain, easing the seedlings from the loose soil and transporting them to the fields. There, with the use of a rounded stick, they set the young plants into prepared hillocks. In the following weeks each hillock was hoed and weeded, and every plant was inspected for worms. As the tobacco matured, field hands topped and suckered each plant. The practice of cutting off the upper bud of the plant, or topping, precluded flowering and encouraged more vigorous growth in the remaining leaves. Removing new shoots that formed at the base of each leaf, or suckering, concentrated growth into the orig-

(pages 22–23)
Fig. 12. Mid-nineteenth-century views of the stages of tobacco cultivation throughout the year, after P. H. Mayo & Brother's "Calendar of Tobacco Cultivation"

MARCH
Protecting the bed with brush

APRIL
Making hills

JULY
TOBACCO CULTURE
Laying by & topping

AUGUST
Worming & suckering

NOVEMBER
Stripping & tying in hands

DECEMBER
Packing for market

inal leaves. During the summer growing season, enslaved workers suckered each tobacco plant two or three times, allowing choice leaves to grow in anticipation of an early fall cutting (see fig. 12). While men and women worked in the tobacco fields throughout the summer, they also spent these months harvesting and processing hemp and reaping grains.

The woody stems of hemp plants contain fibers that were used to make coarse linen cloth as well as rope. While Jefferson expressed a wish that flax and cotton also be grown on the plantation, it appears that hemp became the principal plant fiber raised at Poplar Forest.[25] Extracting the fibers from these plants was hard and disagreeable work involving several steps. First, the plants were allowed to rot, either by placing them in standing water or by laying them out in pastures for several weeks. Once the desired degree of decay had occurred, the hemp was dried, and slaves peeled the stalks by hand, beat them with mallets, or crushed them using a machine known as a brake. Workers then beat the broken fibers with a flat wooden tool, or scutcher, to separate out the unwanted portions of the stem. Following this step, they beat the fibers again and then pulled them through comblike tools, or hatchels, consisting of closely spaced iron teeth. This final step separated out any remaining stem material or dirt and left behind a bundle of long, loose fibers ready to be spun and woven into cloth.

Slaves complained so much of the work required to process hemp that Jefferson discontinued its cultivation for a time. After 1816, however, he installed a horse-powered hemp-brake which he expected would do "the breaking & beating of 10 men."[26]

In Bedford wheat vied with tobacco as the principal cash crop, while slaves cultivated oats for use on the plantation. Harvest occurred from mid-June through early July, a time of intense and grueling work (fig. 13). In 1795 Jefferson described a wheat harvest at one of his Albemarle farms, noting its progress and outlining steps to make the process more efficient. There, teams of young men moved across the fields cutting

FIG. 13. Mid-nineteenth-century sketch of a Virginia wheat harvest by Edwin Forbes

the wheat, while groups of women and boys gathered and bound it. A second team of men stacked and loaded these bundles onto carts to be brought to the barn for storage and treading. The harvest lasted for three days in July, with each man cutting an average of three acres per day. In his notes Jefferson recommended that a blacksmith, seated on a mule cart with his grindstone and spare tools, move constantly through the fields repairing and sharpening scythes, and that two women be assigned as cooks. He saw each person as part of an interrelated harvesting "machine" and felt that with some modifications "the whole machine would move in exact equilibrio."[27]

Following the harvest, slaves threshed the wheat to separate the grain and chaff from the stalk. Before the invention of threshing machines, laborers were obliged to beat the grain with flails against a plank floor, an undertaking which Jefferson described for the processing of clover seed.[28] Laborers saved straw and packed and transported the grain to nearby mills where it would be ground into flour and sold.

Field hands spent the early fall cutting tobacco and hanging it outdoors on scaffolds to dry. Within a few weeks they carried it to tobacco houses and hung it there to cure. Two final tasks relating to the tobacco crop remained in late fall: removing the stems from the dried leaves and packing, or prizing, the leaves into large barrels to be transported to market (see fig. 12). During this time slaves were also busy harvesting corn and fodder, picking pumpkins, digging potatoes, picking and preserving apples and peaches, and making brandy. Late in the season men and women plowed fields and sowed wheat for the following year. Fall and winter were also the time when men slaughtered pigs and cattle, butchered and salted the meat, and hung it to cure.[29]

When not needed to "assist in the crop," artisans followed their own cycles of work. Most plantation industries were tied to the agricultural schedule. Coopers were busiest during the summer and fall, making barrels for transporting tobacco and flour; blacksmiths collected wood from newly cleared fields during the winter months and built charcoal kilns to produce fuel for their shop. Other tasks were spread throughout the year. Will and Hall, the plantation smiths, made nails and tools, shod horses, and repaired broken implements. Bess, Cate, and Maria spun wool, hemp, flax, and cotton to produce cloth, while Edy or Aggy wove it into the coarse cloth characteristic of slave clothing. During the winter in which he was convalescing, Jame Hubbard's son Nace made baskets and shoes.

After 1805, when the construction of Jefferson's octagonal house began, Jerry, Phil Hubbard, and John Hemmings[30] worked with hired artisans in brickmaking, masonry, and carpentry. Through excavation and massive earthmoving, Phil worked to create the sunken south lawn and ornamental mounds. Jame Hubbard's grandson Nace tended Jefferson's vegetable garden, nursery, and landscaped pleasure grounds.[31]

With the coming of winter, the plantation work cycle began anew.

4 Excavations at the Quarter Site

T HE DOCUMENTS THAT preserve information about slavery at Poplar Forest tell only part of its story. They were written, with few exceptions, from the perspective of Jefferson, his overseers, or others who lived outside of the community that enslaved families created. These men were, on the one hand, so familiar with life on the plantation that they did not think it necessary to record the details of slaves' day-to-day existence that interest us today. On the other hand, they did not witness many of the after-hours activities that occurred within the relative privacy of the quarter. Perhaps most importantly, as men raised in a culture distinct from and often at odds with that of the enslaved, they were biased and self-interested observers. As a result, questions raised by modern scholars, such as how people coped with the hardships of slavery, how they exerted control over their daily lives, or, more broadly, how they blended elements of their African past with their current circumstances to create a distinctly African-American culture, are often difficult to answer through documents alone.

Archaeology has provided answers to some basic questions about the lives of enslaved people at Poplar Forest, such as the location and size of housing, the foods that people ate, and the types of objects that they used in daily life. The results of excavations and laboratory analyses also have hinted at the answers to more complex questions about the nature of the community: the ways in which families transformed plantation housing to fit their notions of domestic life, to meet their needs for privacy, and to suit their work habits. Finally, archaeology has contributed to the question of how men and women defined themselves within a system that sought to recast them into a "machine in equilibrio."

Methods

Archaeological evidence provides an alternate view of the past. Except for a few items that have been lost or purposely buried, archaeologists find the objects that people discard and the houses and yards that they have abandoned. People's trash and the ways in which they dispose of it are important and often unique sources of information. Although a writer intentionally chooses the words she scribbles on the page, for example, it is unlikely that she thinks about the information conveyed by the discarded pen. Yet both the pen and the circumstances of its disposal preserve clues about an activity that took place in a certain place and time. They can contain information about the technological development, the sense of style, and even the importance of consumerism within the writer's society. Because the archaeological record is often created unintentionally, it can convey information free from the deliberate biases of its creators.

In spite of this strength, archaeological evidence is not without bias. The preservation of materials in the ground is of real concern when dealing with a site inhabited by people whose material world consisted largely of objects made of wood, cloth, leather, and bone. In the acidic soils of Poplar Forest, bone is only preserved in deposits where the soil acidity has been neutralized by ash or other basic substances. Wood and seeds are only preserved through carbonization. Most other organic materials do not survive at all.

Archaeological data can also be biased by the ways in which they

FIG. 14. Sorting flotation samples in the laboratory

are collected. Although archaeologists typically examine only a part of the sites that they study, they must ensure that their study area is representative of the kinds of activities that occurred across the entire site before they draw broad conclusions. On a smaller scale, if soils are not closely inspected, the information contained in objects such as pins, beads, eggshell fragments, lead shot, fish scales, and bird bones is lost (fig. 14). Aware of these potential problems, archaeologists are careful to sample their sites and the soils within them systematically.

To make sense of the data preserved in the ground, archaeologists must conduct controlled excavations. It is important that information about the context of each artifact and manmade disturbance, or feature, be preserved through detailed field notes, photographs, and drawings. For example, although the eastern half of the quarter at Poplar Forest was subsequently plowed, mixing the soil layers across this part of the

FIG. 15. Archaeologists excavating the quarter site using a ten-foot-grid system

site, the horizontal distribution of artifacts was not significantly affected by plowing. To preserve these horizontal relationships, excavators used a grid of ten-foot squares, further subdivided into five-foot units for collecting artifacts from the plow zone (fig. 15).

Although Poplar Forest archaeologists tested a much larger expanse of ground to find the limits of the site, they completely excavated a continuous area measuring approximately eighty by one hundred feet

FIG. 16. Aerial view of the excavated site looking north. White areas mark the locations of root cellars in structure 1.

(fig. 16). Across the eastern half of the site, digging stopped at a depth of six to eight inches below the surface as excavators reached undisturbed subsoil. Farther west, where later nineteenth-century plowing had not occurred, soil layers survived. Strata formed as plowed soils washed downslope in heavy rains, creating layers of finer, siltier soil that covered earlier deposits. These later layers were carefully excavated to identify strata created by the original occupants of the site.

To recover as many artifacts as possible, excavators screened all soil from the site through one-quarter-inch hardware cloth (fig. 17). Soils associated with cellars, floor surfaces, or layers underneath buildings were wet-screened through finer window mesh to ensure that even the tiniest of objects were found.

By the end of three seasons of excavations, archaeologists had uncovered the remains of a slave settlement. It seems likely that the quarter stretched farther to the east, constructed on land that does not belong

FIG. 17. Screening soil to recover small artifacts

to the museum. Nevertheless, the "footprints" of three structures, their associated yards, and over 20,000 artifacts paint a vivid picture of life at the site in the late eighteenth and early nineteenth centuries.

Domestic Spaces

Excavators found evidence of two periods of plowing at the site. The most recent episode, probably dating to the mid–nineteenth century, created the plow zone that disturbed the quarter's original layers. Evidence of still earlier plowing, sealed beneath the occupation layers of the site, indicates that before becoming home to the quarter site residents, the hillside under investigation was an agricultural field. Successive plantings depleted its soils of nutrients, while continuous plowing of the slope helped to create deep erosion gullies across the face of the hill. By the end of the 1780s, the field was exhausted and badly scarred. No longer valuable agricultural land, it was selected by Jefferson or his overseer as a suitable site for erecting quarters.

In Virginia enslaved carpenters typically used perishable materials to construct dwellings and work spaces. Jefferson noted that it took three carpenters six days to build a slave cabin, "getting the stuff and putting it together." People most often lived adjacent to the fields or shops where they worked. The location of quarters within a plantation periodically changed as fields were exhausted and new land was cleared for cultivation. By ordering that simple and inexpensive cabins be built, planters lessened the costs associated with the regular movement of workers. One such move is documented at Poplar Forest during the winter of 1811. That year, Jefferson transferred a number of slaves from his Tomahawk lands to his Bear Creek farm, advising his overseer that gangs from both communities should work together to provide new housing.[1]

While plantation owners or overseers commonly dictated the locations and sizes of cabins, it seems likely that individuals were free to organize the space around their houses. Men and women enclosed yards, using this outside area as an extension of their living space. Yard activities included domestic chores such as cooking and laundering, while enclosures served to protect gardens and provide privacy. Men and women worked, worshiped, and socialized out-of-doors, leaving behind evidence of their activities in both the physical footprints of fences and cooking pits and the chemical and artifact concentrations that mark the location of trash piles known as middens.

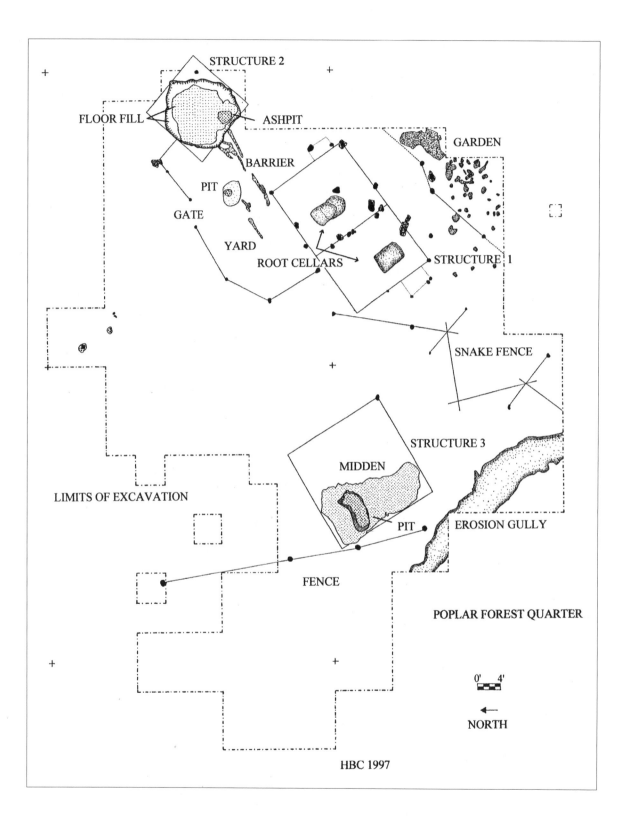

STRUCTURE 2

FLOOR FILL

ASHPIT

BARRIER

PIT

GATE

YARD

ROOT CELLARS

GARDEN

STRUCTURE 1

SNAKE FENCE

STRUCTURE 3

MIDDEN

PIT

EROSION GULLY

LIMITS OF EXCAVATION

FENCE

POPLAR FOREST QUARTER

0'   4'

NORTH

HBC 1997

Structure 1

(opposite page)
FIG. 18. Plan view
of excavated fea-
tures at the quarter

Although small by modern standards, structure 1, measuring approximately fifteen by twenty-five feet, was of a size typical for houses for slaves, free blacks, and middling and poor white farmers of the period (figs. 18 and 19).[2]

The cabin sat on the edge of a gentle slope. It most likely was supported by a stone pier in the northwest corner and by wooden posts set at each remaining corner. Carpenters raised the house on wooden posts positioned at irregular intervals along the north and south walls. Residents replaced the southeast corner post as the building aged.

Like other plantation outbuildings in the region, the cabin probably was built of logs. Documents indicate that at least two other log structures stood at Poplar Forest in the early nineteenth century, and that Jefferson favored log structures to house slaves living at Monticello's Mulberry Row. The archaeological recovery of thousands of structural, roofing, and trim nails within and around the structure confirms that the

FIG. 19. Artist's interpretation of structures 1 and 2 and the work yard connecting them

building was certainly made of wood, while charcoal samples removed from postholes indicate that the supports were fashioned from hickory.[3]

The house was divided into two equal-sized rooms, each measuring twelve and one-half feet by fifteen feet. Chimneys were located on the gable ends of the building, with a single fireplace heating each room. Several pieces of daub found in and around the cabin indicate that carpenters built the chimneys of wood and attempted to fireproof them with a lining of clay.

Each room contained a small pit, or root cellar, set within the floor (fig. 20). The eastern room actually contained two cellars—one dug when the house was built and another dug later to replace it. Unlike northern root cellars, which were designed as walk-in storage places, root cellars associated with southern slave quarters were typically small, rectangular spaces situated beneath cabin floors. Residents sometimes lined them with brick, stone, or wood and covered them with boards or

FIG. 20. Excavated root cellar in the western room of structure 1

a trapdoor set in the wooden floor above.[4] The quarter site root cellars, measuring three by five feet and three by four feet, were simply rectangular pits; no evidence of any lining material was discovered during their excavation.

Root cellars are important elements in understanding slave houses, for unlike the buildings themselves, they were spaces designed by the occupants. Archaeologists disagree about how these spaces were used. Some believe that slaves stored root crops or personal belongings within them. Others feel that they were convenient places for hiding things, either goods stolen from plantation storehouses or objects of spiritual significance that were best kept out of sight.[5]

Multiple cellars are common in seventeenth- and early eighteenth-century quarters, while by the late eighteenth and early nineteenth centuries, many cabins contain only one or two. This trend may reflect a transition in slave housing from barracks-style dwellings, where unrelated people were quartered, to family dwellings. The former might be characterized by many individual storage compartments, while the latter may have contained a single space shared by family members.

A letter written in 1821 suggests one use for cellars at Poplar Forest. That year, carpenter John Hemmings complained in a letter to Thomas Jefferson that Nace was taking all the vegetables from the garden; he "carries them to his cabin and burys them in the ground." He then sold them at the first opportunity.[6] A close examination of the contents of one cellar, in the west room of structure 1, indicates that residents used it to store clothing, tools, and iron hardware. The other two cellars were too badly disturbed by plowing for archaeologists to be sure of their original use.

Found at quarters throughout Virginia, South Carolina, and Tennessee, these features are tangible evidence of a regional custom that may be rooted in West African house design.[7] At the same time, the common occurrence of root cellars suggests that many planters tacitly acknowledged slaves' rights to both property and privacy within their living quarters.

During the years that they were in residence, the cabin's occupants commonly disposed of their household trash by throwing it out of open doors or windows and by dumping it in middens in the yard. Such methods of trash disposal, though jarring to modern sensibilities, were common in the late eighteenth and early nineteenth centuries. Urban shopkeepers and rural farmers, enslaved and free laborers lived at a time when the connection between disease and poor sanitation was not widely understood. It was not until later in the nineteenth century that Victorians began to equate trash not only with disease but with immorality. Out of their worldview, our modern notions of cleanliness and domestic aesthetics emerged.[8]

By studying concentrations of trash disposal, archaeologists determined that a door was located about four feet from the northwest corner of structure 1. A second door probably opened along the northeast half of the cabin as well.

Beyond censuses that enumerate the slaves living at Poplar Forest between 1792 and 1811, there is no evidence to reveal the identities of the occupants of the cabin. The physical division of the house into two rooms, each heated by a chimney and containing its own storage cellar, is consistent with a regional tradition of housing slaves in two-family residences. The practice of using duplexes at Poplar Forest is confirmed by a letter written by overseer Jeremiah Goodman to Thomas Jefferson in 1814. In it Goodman proposed the reorganization of families within an existing dwelling. He declared his intention to build a house for Aggy and give Hannah and her new husband Phil Hubbard "one end of Dick's house." Both Aggy and Hannah were married daughters of Dick and Dinah, and Aggy apparently was sharing their house.[9] Although Jefferson opposed this plan, the letter is important not only because it mentions the use of duplexes, but because it records the practice of housing extended families beneath one roof. It is possible, then, that structure 1 was home to an extended family composed of two distinct households.

Structure 2

Structure 2 sat thirteen feet northeast of structure 1 on a relatively flat piece of ground (see figs. 18 and 19). This building clearly was built of logs. Archaeologists found quantities of burned clay chinking, some pieces still bearing the impressions of the logs they were set against, adjoining the remains of the structure, which may have been associated with a wooden chimney. Structure 2 measured approximately thirteen feet square and faced north, with a door opening along that wall.

The central portion of this structure's earthen floor had been worn into a shallow, bowl-shaped depression by continued use (fig. 21). Archaeologists discovered a small circular pit in the southwest corner of the floor. Packed with soil and concentrated ash, the pit also contained a large stone laid flat, as if someone had placed it there to keep the ash from scattering.

Archaeologists initially believed that the building may have functioned as a meat house or smokehouse, where freshly butchered meat was salted and smoked to preserve it. Samples taken from within the building, however, failed to reveal elevated levels of salts in the soil. Then too, the walls of the ashpit showed no signs of burning, suggesting that the ash was stored but not created here.

Whatever its original purpose, the number and variety of domestic artifacts excavated within and around the structure indicate that for at least part of its life span, the building was home to one or more slaves (fig. 22).

FIG. 21. Excavated floor fill and ashpit of structure 2

Structure 3

Fourteen feet to the north and west of structure 1, archaeologists discovered the corner of a third building (see fig. 18). It had been constructed on one of the steepest parts of the hillside, directly on top of a backfilled erosion gully. Evidence of a wooden support post defined the location of the southeast corner; to provide a level floor, the building must have been raised on piers along its northern face.

Structure 3 measured eighteen and one-half feet per side. Chemical evidence suggests that it had a chimney on the northeastern wall, while artifact concentrations suggest that the door faced north.[10]

An oval pit sat beneath the floor in the southwest corner of the building. Unlike the straight-sided, flat-bottomed root cellars situated beneath the floor of structure 1, this pit resulted from the construction of the building rather than the storage needs of its occupants. It may have been

FIG. 22. Artifacts recovered from the floor of structure 2. *Top left to bottom right*: case bottle fragment, fork tines, wine glass base, buttons, fragments of creamware and pearlware, iron razor, pig jaw fragment.

dug to extract clay used to line a wooden chimney or to provide chinking for walls or mud mortar for stone piers supporting the sill. Whatever its original purpose, it quickly filled with animal bones, broken dishes, and architectural debris once people moved into the building.

Based on the artifacts found in the crawl space beneath the building, along the building's western wall and also in a midden to the north, it seems clear that structure 3 provided housing for one or more people living within the enslaved community. The quality of ceramics found at the building suggests that its occupants enjoyed a slightly higher standard of living than the residents of structure 1, the adjacent cabin. Ceramic evidence, combined with the recovery of some early machine-cut nails, also suggests that structure 3 may have been built slightly later, or occupied slightly longer, than structures 1 and 2 (fig. 23).

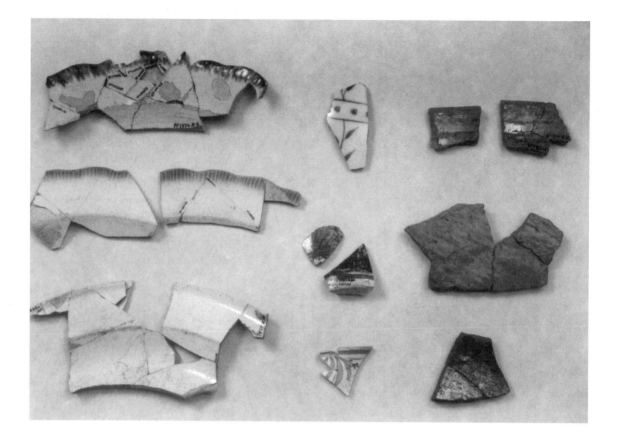

FIG. 23. Pottery recovered from structure 3. *Left to right*: blue- and green-edged pearlware, creamware, painted and annular pearlware, lead-glazed earthenware. The pearlware plate with an even scalloped edge (*left, second from top*) did not come into production until 1810.

Soil Analysis at the Quarter

Most people associate historic artifacts with broken pieces of glass, bent nails, shattered ceramics, discarded animal bones, or other portable objects that were thrown away in the past. Yet other traces of human activity lie hidden in the soil and can be valuable sources of information. *Ecofacts* such as particles of pollen, charred wood fragments, or phytoliths—microscopic plant silicas—provide important clues about the past ecology of a site. Chemicals are another rich source of data. They often can be linked to specific human actions, last in the ground for thousands of years, and do not migrate great distances through the soil.

Archaeologists collect soil samples systematically from layers and features across their sites and map the distributions of certain chemicals contained within them. At the quarter site four principal chemicals were investigated: phosphorus, calcium, potassium, and magnesium. Phosphorus is found in human and animal tissues and waste, and high levels can be associated with animal pens, trash dumps, or privies. Calcium is a component of bone and shell. In the acidic soils of central Virginia, these substances often decompose rapidly, leaving behind only their chemical signatures. High concentrations of calcium may mark the locations of middens, processing areas for meat, or shell walkways. Potassium is found in wood and wood ash and can suggest the placement of hearths or ash deposits. Some archaeologists studying soil chemicals have tentatively linked high magnesium levels in soil to activities associated with burning.[11]

At Poplar Forest soil chemistry has been an important tool in understanding the layout of the quarter. High phosphorus and calcium levels correspond with areas of dense artifact deposition and help to confirm the location and formation of middens. Chemicals suggest that site residents may have deposited certain types of organic waste away from the larger middens where they dumped animal bones and household trash. High potassium levels at the eastern and western ends of structure 1 and along the northeast wall of structure 3 have suggested the location of hearths. Significant variations in chemical levels across relatively short distances have also suggested the location of fences or other aboveground barriers at the site.

Yards

Archaeologists typically discover yard spaces by the fences that surround them, defining their limits and separating within from without. At the quarter excavators uncovered the remains of three barriers dating to the time that the site was inhabited, as well as lines of postholes that may indicate the presence of further fence lines. The first barrier enclosed a space beginning at the northwest wall of structure 1 and extending to the northwest wall of structure 2. Posts, set at ten-foot intervals, anchored panels of wooden uprights, or pickets, forming the outside line of this fence. The line was interrupted by a four-foot-wide gate located midway between the two buildings (see fig. 19).

A second fence defined the southern limit of the yard, stretching between the southwest corner of structure 2 and the east wall of structure 1. Excavators uncovered a series of narrow trenches running in a rough line between the buildings, the only physical remnants of the barrier that once stood there. Clear changes in artifact densities and soil chemical levels in this area indicate that some type of fence divided this space.[12] This barrier may have included a gate for access to the south side of the cabin, although no evidence was found to suggest its location or size.

The yard enclosed by these fences varied from ten to fourteen feet in width and extended to a length of thirty feet. From their front door, residents of the eastern half of structure 1 could enter it directly. Occupants of the western side of that building may have been able to reach the yard through an interior door that connected their living space to that of their neighbors. Others entered the yard through the gate located along its northern boundary. Residents made some effort to keep the yard clear, dumping much of their household trash along and outside of its boundaries. Over time, extensive middens formed along the northern and western sides of the fence.

Residents of the quarter chose to locate this yard on the side of the house facing away from the mansion or overseer's house. This plan allowed them space, air, and light to work in, elements lacking within the dark and crowded buildings. At the same time, the placement of the yard afforded them the freedom to socialize and relax away from the watchful eyes of the overseer and his family.

Archaeologists found evidence of a worm, zigzag, or snake fence

FIG. 24. Early nineteenth-century view by Benjamin Latrobe of an overseer supervising women clearing a new field. Note the snake fence in the background with cross pieces anchoring the locks.

west of structure 1, separating that building from structure 3 (see fig. 18). Fences of this type sat on the surface of the ground and could easily be disassembled and moved.[13] Sometimes carpenters drove opposing pairs of wooden stakes into the ground where the fences locked, a practice which resulted in greater stability. The fence at the quarter site had such stakes, a fact that led to its discovery nearly two hundred years after it was built. Common in colonial Virginia where wood was plentiful, these fences often bordered agricultural fields and pastures (fig. 24).

A series of three postholes located south of structure 1 suggests the location of a fourth fence. This area was remarkably free of artifacts but contained numerous irregular soil disturbances created by plants of varying sizes. Surrounding these planting features was soil rich in chemicals associated with burned wood and decaying organic matter. Such a chemical signature might be left by repeated applications of fertilizing agents such as wood ash and animal dung.[14] Together, these clues suggest that this space was cultivated.

Whether this area served as the site of the residents' vegetable patch or was the edge of a garden associated with the overseer's house located farther to the southeast is not known. There are no direct written references to garden plots cultivated by enslaved men and women at Poplar Forest during Jefferson's ownership, although he did record purchases of fruit and vegetables while visiting the property; the produce may have come from the slaves' gardens. Jefferson also made reference to a "truck patch" which served him as an interim garden until he laid out a more formal space in 1811. Future excavations in this area might allow archaeologists to trace the line of the fence and further define the limits of plantings, a process which might suggest who controlled the plot.[15]

Archaeologists discovered evidence of additional fencing around structure 3. A large part of the yard to the south and west of that building appears to have been roughly paved with local quartz cobbles. Additionally, numerous pieces of blacksmithing slag, material commonly used for paving, were found intermixed with the quartz cobbles. This surface may be associated with a section of road running behind the building, or it may indicate an attempt on the part of the building's occupants to control erosion.

5

The Material World of Slavery

ARCHAEOLOGISTS STUDIED artifact concentrations across the site to help unravel the physical landscape of the quarter. Individual objects or groups of objects provide equally important insights into the material world of slavery. Clearly, the common things that people used and discarded furnish clues to the physical realities of daily life in bondage. At the same time, artifacts hint at the interplay of work and leisure time, the degree of economic freedom that slaves could achieve, and the ways in which men and women defined themselves and their community within the world of the plantation.

Tools

It seems likely that much of slaves' leisure time was taken up, paradoxically, by work. Artifacts provide tangible evidence that there was often no clear distinction between being at work and being at home for enslaved men and women. Indeed, archaeology suggests that some slaves at Poplar Forest, like their contemporaries at other plantations across the South, lived in work spaces.

The meaning of tools found at quarters throughout the Southeast is a source of debate among archaeologists. It has been argued that slaves stole tools and hid them at home as part of a continuous, nonviolent campaign of resistance. While this may be true, there are alternate explanations of why tools are commonly found at quarters: slaves owned them, brought some home for repair or to recycle their parts, and used others to perform tasks that took place where they lived.[1]

Some tools, like bone-handled jackknives or thimbles, clearly belonged to individuals. They formed part of the tool kit of daily living. Historic accounts such as runaway advertisements confirm that many slaves owned and maintained more specialized tools. Shoemakers, carpenters, and other artisans often took their tools with them when they fled from the plantation, helping to ensure that they could practice their trades in freedom.[2] Other implements, like harrows and plows, belonged to the planter and were used communally. These may have been brought to the site for repair or replacement. A number of broken tines, possibly from harrows and hand rakes, appear to have been thrown away at the Poplar Forest quarter once repairs were completed.

Tools found at the site can often be associated with specialized, gender-specific crafts. In a series of memoranda to his overseers, Jefferson outlined the tasks of individuals, enabling modern scholars to understand his concepts of "men's work" and "women's work."[3] Tools and tool parts found at the site and used by male artisans include iron saw files, a gimlet, wedges, croze irons, and a hinge from a folding ruler (fig. 25). Carpenters employed files to sharpen saws, gimlets for making holes, and wedges for splitting or separating wood. Coopers, or barrel-makers, used croze irons to cut the grooves along the inside of staves into which the barrel top and bottom, or heads, were set. Artisans from each of these craft specialties made use of rulers to measure distances. Whether the discovery of these tools means that craftsmen skilled in distinct trades lived at the site, or that an individual collected broken implements to be repaired or recycled, is not known.

FIG. 25. Men's tools found at the quarter. *Top row (right to left)*: unidentified tool (possibly a small smith's hardy), croze irons, hinge for a folding ruler, wedges. *Bottom row*: gimlet and triangular and round files.

Women spun and wove a variety of fibers—including wool, flax, cotton, and hemp—to create the coarse cloth characteristic of slave clothing throughout the Southeast. During the period that the quarter was occupied, this work would have been done in the home. Later, Jefferson authorized the construction of special weaving and spinning houses.

Following the outbreak of hostilities with Great Britain in 1812, Jefferson reminded his overseer that "there will be no chance for negro clothing but what we make ourselves."[4] Scissors, straight pins, and thimbles found near each of the three structures at the quarter suggest that beyond cloth production, women spent much of their time at home sewing for themselves and for their families (fig. 26).

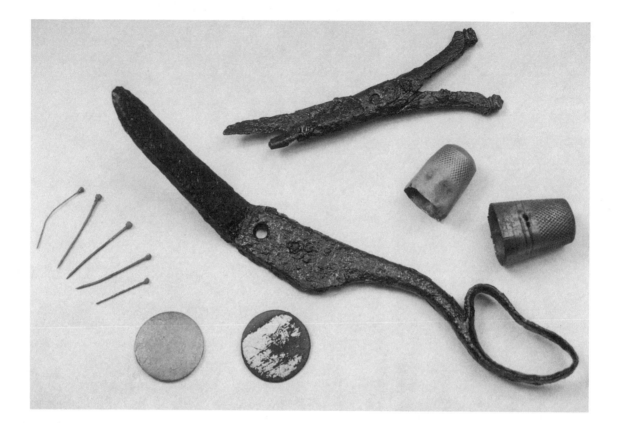

FIG. 26. Women's tools found at the quarter. *Top to bottom*: scissors, thimbles, shears, straight pins, buttons.

Slaves as Consumers

After completing the many domestic chores created by the demands of family life, slaves grew vegetables, raised poultry, made a variety of handicrafts, or performed odd jobs with the intent of earning money (fig. 27). During several visits to Poplar Forest, Jefferson recorded purchasing chickens, ducks, turkeys, and eggs from slave women.[5] He also paid individuals for completing tasks that he believed fell outside the daily round of labor expected of them, such as digging the sunken south lawn in Poplar Forest's landscaped grounds. Those involved in that project were to work "with their own free will" and "in their own time." For his efforts, Phil Hubbard, and perhaps others, received an eighth of a dollar for every cubic yard of earth moved.[6]

Throughout Virginia enslaved men and women not only sold objects

FIG. 27. Coins recovered at the quarter.

Top row: Spanish silver one-eighth real (1790), copper American one-cent piece (1810).

Bottom row: copper American one-cent piece (1808), reverse.

and labor to their owners; they also participated in an informal economy with neighboring plantations, providing goods or services in exchange for money, store credits, or assistance. Additionally, some Virginia slaves were able to carry merchandise to local stores to sell for "ready money" and there purchased a variety of goods. The surviving account books of merchants operating stores in Bedford, Buckingham, Franklin, Fauquier, and Orange counties provide a glimpse into the economic lives of enslaved men and women from 1771 through 1817. Men outnumbered women by a large margin as store customers, although clearly much of what they purchased was intended for the use of their wives and children.[7]

Will, living at Poplar Forest, purchased rum, buttons, thread, and cloth from a New London store in 1772 (fig. 28). Slaves from other plantations in Bedford and Campbell counties purchased ribbons, handkerchiefs, hats, shoes, stockings, blankets, knives, pots, dishes, padlocks, combs, a looking glass, awls, cotton or wool cards, needles, pins, scis-

FIG. 28. Page from the ledger of Bedford County merchant John Hook, showing the account of Poplar Forest slave Will

sors and thimbles, sugar, molasses, cider, and whiskey. Cloth and items associated with clothing were most commonly purchased. Slave customers paid their debts with cash, crops, baskets and brooms, and their own labor.[8]

At the quarter site archaeologists found a variety of personal items that may have been obtained by individual purchases. Among the most common discoveries were clothing accessories (fig. 29). The quantity of these objects suggests the importance of personal adornment among slaves and their awareness of and ability to keep pace with changing fashions. One hundred and twenty-two buttons, thirty-five glass beads, a fragment of a gilt chain, an aiglet or lace tip, and six fancy buckles (used to fasten shoes, breeches, hatbands, and hair ribbons) were scattered within the three structures and in their adjoining yards. In a plantation community where many goods were rationed and where everyone's clothing was literally cut from the same cloth, the Poplar Forest slaves valued clothing accessories and jewelry as important tools of self-expression and community identity. The choice they made to use some of their limited economic resources to obtain adornment objects argues strongly for the importance of such items within the community.

Men and women ornamented their clothing and themselves to display personal taste, to attract potential spouses, and to celebrate important events in their lives, adapting European materials and American contexts to a cultural practice that had its roots in Africa. Clothing played an important symbolic role in helping slaves to cross the lines between work and leisure, routine and holiday, secular and sacred (figs. 30 and 31).[9]

While the residues of activities relating to work are common finds at quarters, it is much more difficult to discover and to interpret evidence of the many ways that slaves chose to relax. Documents and oral testimonies from former slaves indicate that music and storytelling were important components of life "after hours." Residents and visitors gath-

(opposite page)
FIG. 29. Adornment items recovered at the quarter, including a variety of buckle types and sizes, fancy and common buttons, beads, a lace tip, and a pierced stone ornament (*upper right*).

FIG. 30. Benjamin Latrobe's watercolor of men having their hair styled in late eighteenth-century Virginia

FIG. 31. Lewis Miller's 1853 watercolor of a slave dance in Lynchburg, Virginia, showing the variety of adornment items worn by men and women

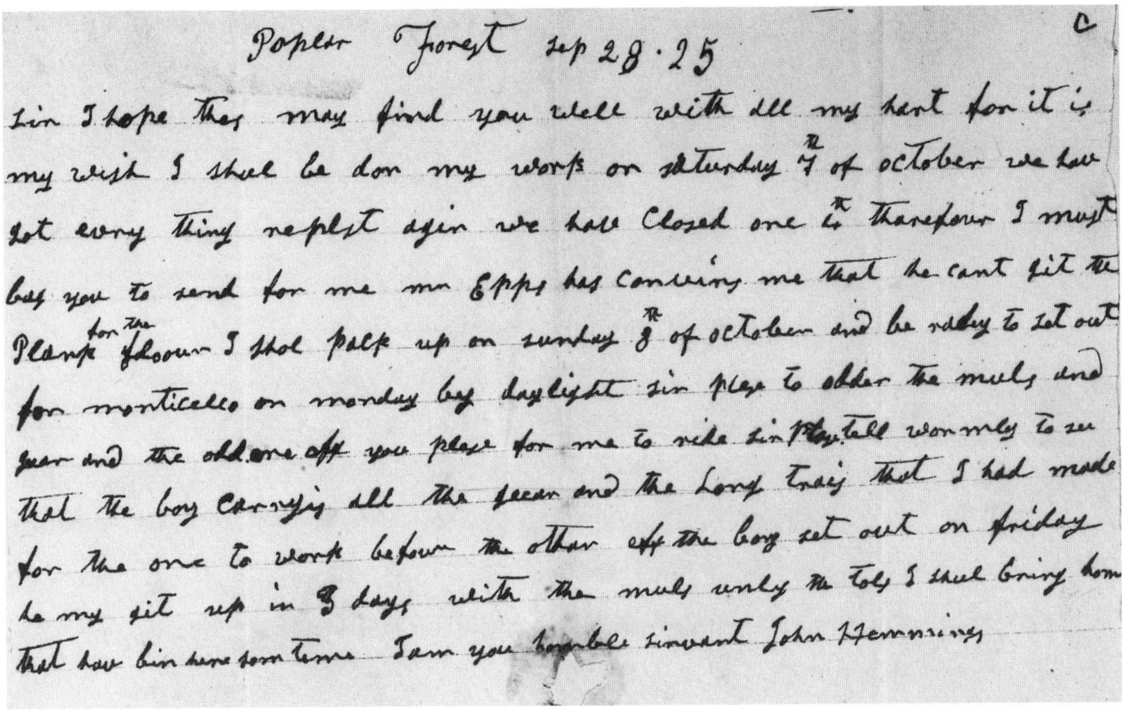

Poplar Forest sep 28·25

Sir I hope thes may find you well with all my hart for it is my wish I shall be don my works on saturday 1 of october we have got every thing replst agin we have Closed one in tharefour I must bag you to send for me mr Epps has conwins me that he cant git the Plank for the floour I shall palk up on sunday 8 of october and be redy to set out for monticello on monday by daylight sir plas to odder the muls and gear and the old one aff you plase for me to ride sin play tell wommly to see that the boy carrys all the geear and the Long tools that I had made for the one to work before the other aff the boy set out on friday he my git up in 3 days with the muls unly the tols I shall bring hom that have bin here som time I am you humble sirvant John Hemmings

FIG. 32. Letter written by John Hemmings to Thomas Jefferson discussing his schedule

ered in the evening and on Sundays to share a drink and a game of cards, pass along news and gossip, or relax with a leisurely smoke.

Artifacts only hint at the range of leisure activities. Two homemade clay marbles are the only preserved remnants of toys and games played at the site. Most toys were likely made of cloth, leather, paper, or wood and have not survived. Fragments of a writing slate may have been part of an artisan's tool kit or may have been used by a resident of the site as he or she learned to read and write. Although formal education was denied to slaves during this period, John Hemmings, who did much of the carpentry for Jefferson at Poplar Forest, and Hannah, the cook, are known to have been literate, because letters written in their hand survive (fig. 32).[10] It is likely that others, particularly craftsmen and women, needed some degree of literacy to perform their work effectively. Bent over writing slates in the yards and doorways of the quarter, these men and women might have shared their knowledge with others.

Jefferson gave women an iron pot at the time of their marriage if they chose a spouse from within the plantation community. While designed for cooking, these pots fulfilled another role in the quarter. Across the South testimonies of former slaves refer to the custom of overturning iron pots or filling them with water during gatherings. Both water and iron had powerful spiritual associations in West Africa, and many slaves believed that these elements together protected the community from outsiders by muffling the sounds of their meetings.[11]

African Americans, like other Virginians, were habitual smokers, and clay smoking pipes are commonly found on domestic sites. At the Poplar Forest quarter, archaeologists found a variety of pipes, ranging from English tobacco pipes to green-glazed pipes made in Virginia and North Carolina with bowls molded in the form of an Indian head. They were found in root cellars, beneath the floor of structure 3, and in middens along the work-yard fence.

In addition to these mass-produced smoking implements, archaeologists discovered fragments of tobacco pipes at the site made from micaceous schist, a soft stone common to central Virginia. Complete pipes are elbow-shaped and were smoked using a reed as a stem. While the majority of the pipe pieces are plain, several fragments bear decorations of incised parallel lines, crosses, or areas of cross-hatching (fig. 33). One pipestem is octagonal in shape. In addition to stone fragments of bowls and stems, excavators also found a piece of stone that appears to be a blank from which the maker intended to form a finished pipe. Like the whole pipes, the blank is elbow-shaped, and it had holes drilled through each section to form the bowl and stem of the pipe. While being drilled to create one of these holes, the stone broke, and the blank was discarded.

Archaeologists found further remnants of pipe wasters. Some pieces of schist waste were cubical, while others were flat and show clear cut marks along their sides. Taken together, these seemingly insignificant fragments confirm that not only were stone pipes used at the site, but they were made there.[12]

FIG. 33. Decorations incised on pieces of stone pipes found at the quarter site

Without excavation of the quarter site, the existence of this craft at Poplar Forest would have been unknown, as no surviving documents hint that pipemaking was among the skills of plantation residents. In spite of the rigorous demands of daily life, the maker or makers found time to gather raw materials, carve and finish pipes, and in some cases decorate them. They are rare examples of workmanship and aesthetic values preserved within an early nineteenth-century slave context. Indeed, although small numbers of similar stone pipes have been found on other sites at Poplar Forest, Monticello, Jefferson's birthplace Shadwell, and the site of an early nineteenth-century stable in Lynchburg, Virginia, the collection from the quarter site is the largest and most varied ever found in Virginia.

Dining and Food

Ceramic storage and serving vessels, cast-iron cooking pots, burned seed remains, and animal bones provide a wealth of information about diet and nutrition among residents of the quarter. At the same time, these objects comment on other aspects of life, from economic status to social relations between blacks and whites on the plantation.

Broken fragments of English, Virginian, and perhaps North Carolinian pottery are some of the most common artifacts found at the quarter (fig. 34). During the late eighteenth and early nineteenth centuries, potters working in factories in the English Midlands mass-produced ceramic vessels that were sold around the world. An analysis of the forms of ceramic vessels provides information about the ways in which food was stored and served at the quarter, while the study of decorations can be helpful in dating individual pieces and in determining their relative costs. Much less is currently known about the American-made ceramics, since fewer records from this period survive relating to potters working in the piedmont region of the upper South.

Not surprisingly, the ceramics that archaeologists found at the site were among the most inexpensive wares available on the market during the late eighteenth and early nineteenth centuries. During this period manufacturers priced refined English earthenware by decoration. The more labor-intensive transfer-printed wares were the most expensive, while undecorated or edge-decorated wares were the least costly.[13] Most

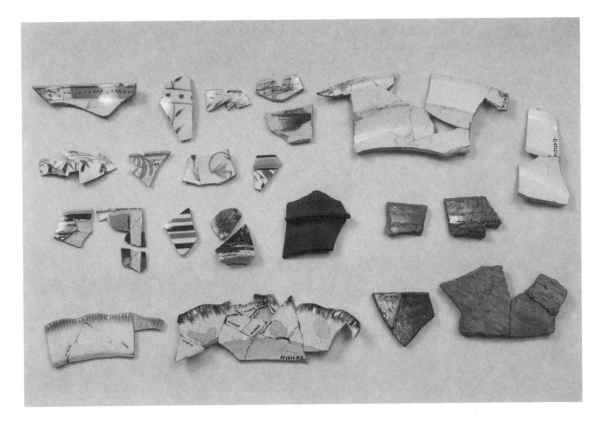

FIG. 34. Ceramic types found at the quarter, including English wares and American pottery. *Left and top right*: painted, annular, and shell-edged pearlware, creamware, black basalt. *Bottom right*: lead-glazed earthenware.

of the vessels at the site fell at the bottom of the price scale. The occupants of structure 1 appear to have used the least-expensive wares, while those of structure 3 set their table with slightly more costly pieces. Several of the locally made vessels were underfired or suffered from defects in the glaze, suggesting that slaves bought, or were given, potters' seconds.

Residents of the quarter site stored food in stoneware and earthenware pots, in glass bottles, and probably in other containers made of biodegradable materials. They dried, pickled, or brandied fruits and vegetables to preserve them throughout the winter.

Intermixed with the soil filling one root cellar in structure 1 and covering the floor of structure 2, an assortment of discarded animal bones and burned plant remains preserves information about diet and the means by which people obtained their food (fig. 35). Occupants of the site consumed beef, pork, venison, opossum, rabbit, chicken, turkey,

FIG. 35. Artifacts related to hunting and diet, including animal bone, a gunflint, lead shot, walnut shells, and a peach pit.

and fish. They also ate a variety of fruits, vegetables, and nuts. Those preserved archaeologically include fruit seeds and pits from grapes, raspberries, cherries, peaches, huckleberries and persimmons; vegetable and grain remains from beans, corn, wheat, and sunflowers; and nut shells from hickory and black walnut trees. Together, plant remains from the site suggest that slaves had access to fresh fruits and vegetables grown in garden plots and gathered from surrounding fields and woods.[14]

Thomas Jefferson recorded that overseers provided food rations of pork, salt fish, corn, wheat, salt, and whiskey to the slaves annually and at harvesttime. The bones from the site indicate that residents received mostly heads, backbones, and feet of domesticated cattle and pigs, cut from the less meaty parts of the animal. Bones from the wild species at the site, on the other hand, represent a diversity of body parts, suggesting that individuals controlled this meat supply through a combination

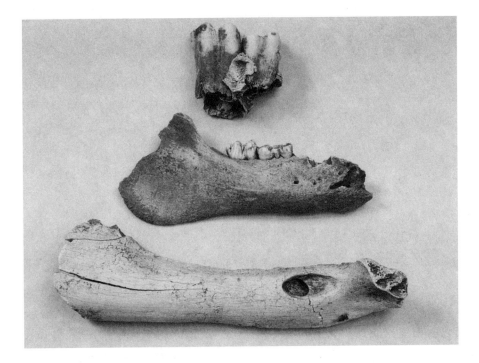

Fig. 36. Animals consumed at the quarter included domesticated cattle (*top*) and pig (*center*) and wild species such as white-tailed deer (*bottom*).

of hunting and trapping which occurred outside the plantation provisioning system (fig. 36). Pieces of lead shot (some that clearly had been fired) and a single gunflint confirm that one or more African Americans living at the site had access to firearms and used them to obtain fresh meat (see fig. 35).[15]

The connection between slaves and guns grows more interesting when put into a larger context. During the years that the quarter site was occupied, whites throughout the American South and the Caribbean increasingly feared slave insurrections. A slave revolt at the close of the eighteenth century resulted in the creation of the Republic of Haiti in 1804, while closer to home, Gabriel Prosser led a failed slave rebellion in and around Richmond, Virginia, during the summer of 1800.[16] The residents of Poplar Forest, both black and white, must have been aware of growing tensions in local communities. However this drama played out in the day-to-day interactions of the plantation, it does not seem to have precluded slaves' access to firearms.

Privacy

The study of the quarter site has provided an obvious—but important
—insight: the conditions of slavery at Poplar Forest left scant room for
privacy. People had little choice in where they would live or who would
be their neighbors. Dwellings, most often shared with family members,
were crowded, small, and close together. Yards were also shared. Even
trash piles, situated in the open air, were communal and available for in-
spection. Owners and overseers scrutinized slaves at work for signs of
illness, disobedience, or rebellion, while at home people inevitably ob-
served each other, quarreled, and gossiped. There were few moments
of solitude in the quarters and fewer secrets.

As documents indicate, the Poplar Forest community was in a state
of flux from the 1770s through the early 1790s. Men and women arrived,
settled, and moved on, often within the span of a few years. People
shared the quarters with family, friends, and strangers. This social instability must inevitably have led to a certain degree of tension. Even
during the relatively stable years after 1790, movements between plantations introduced new faces to the quarters, as free workmen arrived
to build Jefferson's octagonal house, enslaved laborers and artisans arrived from Albemarle to help in its construction, and new overseers
were hired to manage day-to-day plantation affairs.

Men and women addressed the instability or mistrust that periodically arose within their community in a variety of ways. When disputes
arose between individuals that could not be settled, one or both parties
appealed to Jefferson for resolution. Phil Hubbard ran away to Monticello to state his case before his owner because the overseer would not
recognize his marriage to Hannah. Similarly, John Hemmings, unable
to stop Nace's forays into the garden, turned to Jefferson to establish
control.

On a daily basis bondspeople avoided confrontations in both subtle

FIG. 37. Archaeologists discovered a variety of lock parts at the site, including this complete padlock and several well-preserved keys.

and obvious ways. One strategy discovered through archaeology was their use of locks (fig. 37). To safeguard their belongings and their limited privacy from overseers, workmen, neighbors, and family members, some Bedford County slaves purchased locks.[17]

Archaeologists have interpreted locks and keys, like other artifacts, as evidence in broader historical debates concerning such topics as resistance or the retention of West African practices in the New World. One argument has suggested that locks found on quarter sites are the by-products of theft, deposited by slaves who broke into plantation storehouses to take food or tools and carried the evidence away with them to hide. An alternate hypothesis, concerning keys rather than locks, suggests that enslaved musicians may have used these objects to make traditional music.[18] At the Poplar Forest quarter, archaeologists found both locks and keys—one complete padlock, parts of at least nine additional padlocks, two box locks (for doors or chests), and four keys.

Together, these suggest a more literal interpretation—their use for securing doors, chests, cupboards, and other spaces where people kept personal belongings.

Though common objects, locks convey important information about relationships within and between the quarter and the larger plantation. Like coins, fancy buckles, or tools, they confirm that slaves owned objects of value, things that were worth protecting. Their presence in such quantities at the site also suggests that Jefferson and his overseers accepted slaves' right to property and to a degree of privacy. The extent of these rights may have been subject to negotiation, but the locks confirm that they were recognized and respected.

6 Conclusions

ARTIFACTS FOUND ON the site suggest that sometime after 1810 the quarter was abandoned and its residents moved to new housing elsewhere on the plantation. It is possible that the site's abandonment corresponds with the movement of slaves to Bear Creek in the winter of 1811. It seems more likely, however, that the site fell victim to larger changes occurring on the plantation the following year. During the winter of 1812, slaves were instructed to begin laying out the fences for Jefferson's curtilage, a sixty-one-acre enclosure surrounding his newly completed house.[1] The creation of a curtilage was only part of a larger restructuring of the plantation landscape brought about during Jefferson's retirement. Old fields were abandoned or their boundaries recast, new fields were opened up in the virgin lands beyond the south branch of Tomahawk Creek, and a new road was laid connecting Jefferson's residence to the outside world. The focus of activities shifted from the "Old plantation" to the new, resulting in the abandonment and destruction of the quarters.

Many questions remain to be answered about slavery at Poplar Forest. However, recent excavations have provided the first clear view of life in the quarters. Through archaeology, we can begin to piece together the layout of the early plantation landscape, including the size and relationships of slaves' dwellings, work spaces, and yards (fig. 38). Artifacts such as coins, buttons, pipes, gunflints, and padlocks found

FIG. 38. This exhibit building stands above the site of the duplex cabin excavated at the quarter and is used to interpret the site to visitors.

within the site have challenged popular views of slavery, suggesting the ways in which people made choices and exerted control over their lives. While documents record that residents resisted enslavement through theft, work slowdowns, flight, and violence, the archaeological record best reflects more subtle forms of day-to-day resistance to the dehumanizing influence of slavery.

Much of the story of the African-American community living at Poplar Forest still remains buried in the ground. We do not yet know where the families who called the quarter home during the opening decade of the nineteenth century went to live in the years following its destruction. Nor do we understand the full impact of Jefferson's retirement years upon the lives of the men and women who served him in

Bedford. Yet the study of this single site, with its soil stains and its thousands of fragments of bone, seeds, tools, ceramics, and other common objects, is an important first step in coming to understand how individuals and families at Poplar Forest shaped their lives within the confines of slavery.

Notes

1. Introduction

1. Chambers, *Poplar Forest and Jefferson*, 2; TJ to Benjamin Rush, Aug. 17, 1811, DLC.

2. Chambers, *Poplar Forest and Jefferson*, 8–11.

2. Finding "The Old Plantation"

1. "Marriage Settlement for Martha Jefferson," in Boyd, *Papers of Thomas Jefferson* 16:190; "Poplar Forest," ViU; "Survey of Jefferson's Tract of 4,000 Acres," CsmH; "Poplar Forest Survey," private collection; Lounsbury, *Glossary of Early Southern Architecture and Landscape*, 222–23.

3. The Enslaved Community at Poplar Forest

1. Marmon, "Poplar Forest Research Report," 3:2.

2. Malone, *Jefferson and His Time* 1:161–63; Chambers, *Poplar Forest and Jefferson*, 4–5; Marmon, "Poplar Forest Research Report," 1:8.

3. Malone, *Jefferson and His Time* 1:441–45.

4. Betts, *Farm Book*, 7.

5. Ibid., 8, 15–18, 24.

6. TJ to Thomas Mann Randolph, Feb. 4, 1790, MHi; Stanton, *Slavery at Monticello*, 16.

7. John Hemmings to TJ, Nov. 29, 1821, MHi; Jeremiah Goodman to TJ, Dec. 30, 1814, ViU; Betts, *Garden Book*, 539–40; Betts, *Farm Book*, 483.

8. Betts, *Farm Book*, 42–44.

9. TJ and Reuben Perry Deed, Feb. 1811, ViW; TJ to Bernard Peyton, Jan. 5, 1824, MHi.

10. Betts, *Garden Book*, 539–40; Betts, *Farm Book*, 16, 24, 30, 57, 60, 129; "Slave Schedule c. 1811," PPRF.

11. Heath, "Notes on Marriage Patterns."

12. Joel Yancey to TJ, Oct. 14, 1819, TJ to Joel Yancey, Jan. 11, 1818, MHi; Jeremiah Goodman to TJ, Dec. 30, 1814, ViU; TJ to Jeremiah Goodman, Dec. 10, 1814, MoSHi; TJ to Patrick Gibson, Dec. 24, 1813, DLC; Stanton, *Slavery at Monticello*, 38–40; Bear, *Jefferson at Monticello*, 62–63; Reuben Perry to TJ, Dec. 23, 1809, ViW.

13. Betts, *Garden Book*, 466, 492; TJ to Goodman, March 5, 1813, DLC.

14. Betts, *Farm Book*, 46 (teens as gatherers), 77 (children as nurses); TJ to George Jeffreys, March 3, 1817, DLC (boys as field laborers); Betts, *Garden Book*, 357–58, 465–67, 487–88, 492–93 (children and teens at PF), 465–67 (adults at PF). See also Fogel, *Without Consent or Contract*, 53–55; Joyner, "World of the Plantation Slaves," 52, 56, 57; Bear, *Jefferson at Monticello*, 62–63; TJ to Jeremiah Goodman, March 5, 1813, DLC; TJ to Joel Yancey, Jan. 11, 1818, and to Edmund Bacon, Nov. 29, 1817, MHi (young people going to Monticello for training); Joel Yancey to TJ, Aug. 29, 1816, and TJ to Mr. Colelaser, Aug. 8, 1817, MHi (PF carpenters and coopers); Betts, *Farm*

Book, 77, and Stanton, *Slavery at Monticello*, 24 (older slaves).

15. Betts, *Garden Book*, 465–67; "Survey of Jefferson's Tract of 4,000 Acres," CsmH; "Poplar Forest Survey," private collection.

16. Mary Lewis to TJ, April 14, 1790, ViU (measles); Betts, *Garden Book*, 465–67 (pleurisies, fevers, dysenteries, and venereal cases); Joel Yancey to TJ, Jan. 9, 1819, MHi (dysentery, bowel complaints, ruptures); Joel Yancey to TJ, Feb. 27, 1820, MHi (whooping cough); TJ to William Steptoe, Dec. 8, 1815, ViU (fevers); Steptoe Account with TJ, 1813–14, ViU (accidents and infections); TJ to Joel Yancey, Jan. 17, 1819, and Joel Yancey to TJ, Jan. 18, 1819, MHi (child care); Joel Yancey to TJ, Jan. 9, 1819, MHi (complications of childbirth). See also Savitt, *Medicine and Slavery*.

17. Steptoe Account with TJ, 1813–14, ViU; Betts, *Garden Book*, 465–67.

18. Joel Yancey to TJ, July 1, 1819, MHi. See also Savitt, *Fevers, Agues, and Cures*, 48; Sobel, *The World They Made Together*, 171–77.

19. Edwards-Ingram, "African-American Medicinal and Health Practices," 68–71.

20. Savitt, *Fevers, Agues, and Cures*, 22–24; Raymer, "Macroplant Remains," 16–17.

21. Betts, *Garden Book*, 465–67, 492–93, 517–18; TJ to Joel Yancey, July 18, 1815, MHi. See also Boyd, *Papers of Thomas Jefferson* 7:209–12; Breen, *Tobacco Culture*, 46–55; Andrews, "Inside Archaeology," 28–29.

22. Betts, *Garden Book*, 517–18; Joel Yancey to TJ, May 22, 1821, TJ to Archibald Robertson, May 25, 1822, MHi.

23. Betts, *Garden Book*, 465–67, 492–93, 517–18.

24. Ibid., 465–67.

25. Ibid., 465–67, 492–93, 517–18.

26. Betts, *Farm Book*, 252–53. See also Evans, *East Anglian Linen Industry*, 16–27.

27. Betts, *Farm Book*, 46.

28. Betts, *Garden Book*, 488–89, 539–40; TJ to Joel Yancey, June 7, 1815, MHi.

29. TJ to Martha Randolph, Aug. 31, 1815, Joel Yancey to TJ, Dec. 12, 1819, MHi; Andrews, "Inside Archaeology," 28–29.

30. I have chosen to spell the enslaved carpenter's name *Hemmings* rather than the more commonly used *Hemings* because that is the spelling he used in his letters.

31. Chambers, *Poplar Forest and Thomas Jefferson*, 37, 41–42, 45–47, 53, 67, 70, 105, 107, 111, 114, 115, 118, 121, 123, 125, 129–31, 136, 143–44, 157–59 (Jerry, Hubbard, Hemmings); Betts, *Farm Book*, 42–44, and John Hemmings to TJ, Nov. 2, 1819, Nov. 29, 1821, MHi (Nace).

4. Excavations at the Quarter Site

1. Betts, *Farm Book*, 67; Betts, *Garden Book*, 465–67.

2. Sobel, *The World They Made Together*, 100–104; Upton, "White and Black Landscapes," 361.

3. TJ to Jeremiah Goodman, Oct. 10, 1812, PPAMP; TJ to William Newby, Jan. 20, 1815, DLC; Kelso, "Archaeology of Slave Life at Monticello," 8–9; Raymer, "Macroplant Remains," 18.

4. Singleton, "Archaeology of Slave Life," 166–67.

5. Kelso, *Kingsmill Plantations*, 104–5, 120, 201; Sprinkle, "Charles Cox's Mill House Chest," 91–93; Samford, "Archaeology of African-American Slavery," 95; Samford, "Strong Is the Bond of Kinship."

6. John Hemmings to TJ, Nov. 29, 1821, MHi.

7. Yentsch, "Below-Ground 'Storage Cellars' among the Ibo," 3–4.

8. South, *Method and Theory in Historical Archaeology*, 47–50; King, "Comparative Midden Analysis," 17–39; King and Miller, "View from the Midden," 37–59; Kelso, "Archaeology of Slave Life at Monticello," 6, 11–12.

9. Jeremiah Goodman to TJ, Dec. 30, 1814, ViU; Kelso, "Archaeology of Slave Life at Monticello," 10, 12.

10. Fischer, "Chemical Analysis of Soils," 19.

11. Ibid., 3–4.

12. Ibid., 24.

13. Betts, *Garden Book*, 492–93.

14. Fischer, "Chemical Analysis of Soils," 24–25; Spurrier, *Practical Farmer*, 35, 41.

15. Bear and Stanton, *Jefferson's Memorandum Books*, 1260, 1357; Betts, *Garden Book*, 464–65. See also Stanton, *Slavery at Monticello*, 38; Sobel, *The World They Made Together*, 111; Upton, "White and Black Landscapes," 367; Moore, "Afro-American Foodways in Early Virginia," 74–75; Vlatch, "Plantation Landscapes of the Antebellum South," 25.

5. The Material World of Slavery

1. Kelso, "Archaeology of Slave Life at Monticello," 14. See also Mullin, *Africa in America*, 152.

2. Smith and Wojtowicz, *Blacks Who Stole Themselves*, 151; Windley, *Runaway Slave Advertisements* 1:73, 137, 193, 230, 307–8, 383, 2:264, 3:8, 446, 466, 555, 694–95.

3. Betts, *Garden Book*, 465–67; Betts, *Farm Book*, 77.

4. TJ to Jeremiah Goodman, Aug. 9, 1812, DLC.

5. Bear and Stanton, *Jefferson's Memorandum Books*, 511, 1295, 1313, 1338.

6. TJ to Hugh Chisolm, June 5, 1807, MHi. See also Stanton, *Slavery at Monticello*, 27, 38; Ann Cary Randolph Account Book, 1806–8, DLC.

7. Heath, "Slavery and Consumerism," 6; Hook Petty Ledger, 1771–76, and Hook Account Book, 1788–1808, NcD; Merchandise Accounts, Buckingham County, 1797–98, Ledgers of Blackwell and Pickett, 1803–10, and Barbour and Johnson Daybook, 1785–86, ViU.

8. Hook Petty Ledger; Hook Account Book; Davis and Preston Daybook, 1817, ViU; Blackwell and Pickett Ledgers; Mullin, *Africa in America*, 152; Martin, *Buying into the World of Goods*, 306–9; Schlotterbeck, "Internal Economy of Slavery," 170–81.

9. Heath, "Buttons, Beads, and Buckles."

10. Hannah to TJ, Nov. 15, 1818, MHi. Eight letters from John Hemmings to Thomas Jefferson regarding work at Poplar Forest are in the MHi collections: Oct. 20, Nov. 2, 18, Dec. 2, 8, 1819, Nov. 29, 1821, Sept. 18, 28, 1825. See also John Hemmings to Septimia Randolph, Aug. 28, 1825, ViU; Stanton, *Slavery at Monticello*, 40–41.

11. Perdue et al., *Weevils in the Wheat*, 93, 119, 141, 161, 196, 198, 203, 214, 217, 230, 242.

12. Canel, "Poplar Forest's Schist Smoking Pipes."

13. Miller, "Classification and Economic Scaling," 1–40; Miller, "Revised Set of CC Index Values," 1–25.

14. Andrews, "Faunal Analysis of Slave Quarter Site"; Andrews, "Faunal Analysis for Feature 1206"; Raymer, "Macroplant Remains."

15. Sanford, "Archaeology of Plantation Slavery in Piedmont Virginia," 126, 128, table 8.3; Pogue and White, "House for Families' Slave Quarter Site," 41; Thompson, "Private Life of the Mount Vernon Slaves," 17–19.

16. Egerton, *Gabriel's Rebellion*.

17. Hook Account Book; Upton, "White and Black Landscapes," 367.

18. Kelso, "Archaeology of Slave Life at Monticello," 14; Samford, "Archaeology of African-American Slavery," 110–11.

6. Conclusions

1. Betts, *Garden Book*, 492–93.

Bibliography

Manuscript Sources

American Philosophical Society, Philadelphia (PPAMP)
  Jefferson Papers
Duke University, Special Collections Library (NcD)
  John Hook Papers: Hook Petty Ledger, 1771–76; Account Book, 1788–1808
Huntington Library, San Marino, Calif. (CsmH)
  Jefferson Papers
Jones Memorial Library, Lynchburg, Va.
  Lynchburg Account Book, 1796
Library of Congress, Washington, D.C. (DLC)
  Jefferson Papers
Massachusetts Historical Society, Boston (MHi)
  Jefferson Papers
Missouri Historical Society, St. Louis (MoSHi)
  Jefferson Papers
Rosenbach Library and Museum, Philadelphia (PPRF)
  Jefferson Papers
Swem Library, College of William and Mary, Williamsburg, Va. (ViW)
  Trist Papers
University of Virginia Library, Charlottesville (ViU)
  Barbour Family Papers: Barbour and Johnson Daybook, 1785–86
  Blackwell and Pickett, Ledgers, 1803–10
  Davis and Preston Daybook, 1817
  Edgehill-Randolph Papers
  Jefferson Papers
  Merchandise Accounts, Buckingham County, 1797–98

Published Sources and Reports

Andrews, Susan Trevarthen. "Faunal Analysis for Poplar Forest: Feature 1206." MS on file, Thomas Jefferson's Poplar Forest. Forest, Va., 1995.
———. "Faunal Analysis of Slave Quarter Site at Poplar Forest." MS on file, Thomas Jefferson's Poplar Forest. Forest, Va., 1994.
———. "Inside Archaeology: The Archaeology Lab and How to Make Bones Talk." *Notes on the State of Poplar Forest* 2 (1994): 25–30.
Bear, James A. Jr., ed. *Jefferson at Monticello*. Charlottesville, Va., 1967.
Bear, James A. Jr., and Lucia Stanton, eds. *Jefferson's Memorandum Books: Accounts, with Legal Records and Miscellany, 1767–1826*. 2 vols. *The Papers of Thomas Jefferson*, 2d ser. Princeton, N.J., 1997.
Betts, Edwin Morris, ed. *Thomas Jefferson's Farm Book*. Rept. Charlottesville, Va., 1987.
———. *Thomas Jefferson's Garden Book*. Philadelphia, 1944.
Boyd, Julian P., et al., eds. *The Papers of Thomas Jefferson*. 27 vols. to date. Princeton, N.J., 1950—.

Breen, T. H. *Tobacco Culture: The Mentality of the Great Tidewater Planters on the Eve of Revolution*. Princeton, N.J., 1985.

Campbell, Edward D. C. Jr., with Kym S. Rice, ed. *Before Freedom Came: African-American Life in the Antebellum South*. Charlottesville, Va., 1991.

Canel, Hannah B. "Poplar Forest's Schist Smoking Pipes." MS on file, Thomas Jefferson's Poplar Forest. Forest, Va., 1996.

Chambers, S. Allen, Jr. *Poplar Forest and Thomas Jefferson*. Forest, Va., 1993.

Edwards-Ingram, Ywone. "An Inter-Disciplinary Approach to African-American Medicinal and Health Practices in Colonial America." *Watermark* 20, no. 3 (1997): 67–73.

Egerton, Douglas R. *Gabriel's Rebellion: The Virginia Slave Conspiracies of 1800 and 1802*. Chapel Hill, N.C., 1993.

Evans, Nesta. *The East Anglian Linen Industry, Rural Industry, and Local Economy, 1500–1800*. Brookfield, Vt., 1985.

Fischer, Lisa E. "Report on the Chemical Analysis of Soils at the Poplar Forest Quarter Site." MS on file, Thomas Jefferson's Poplar Forest. Forest, Va., 1996.

Fogel, Robert William. *Without Consent or Contract: The Rise and Fall of American Slavery*. New York, 1989.

Franklin, Maria, and Garrett R. Fesler, eds. *Historical Archaeology and Current Perspectives on Ethnicity*. Williamsburg, Va. (forthcoming).

Heath, Barbara J. "Buttons, Beads, and Buckles: Contextualizing Adornment within the Bounds of Slavery." In *Historical Archaeology and Current Perspectives on Ethnicity*, ed. Maria Franklin and Garrett R. Fesler. Williamsburg, Va. (forthcoming).

——. "Slavery and Consumerism: A Case Study from Central Virginia." *African-American Archaeology: Newsletter of the African-American Archaeology Network* 19 (1997): 1–8.

——. "Notes on Marriage Patterns." MS on file, Thomas Jefferson's Poplar Forest. Forest, Va., 1996.

Joyner, Charles. "The World of the Plantation Slaves." In *Before Freedom Came: African-American Life in the Antebellum South*, ed. Edward D. C. Campbell Jr. with Kym S. Rice, 51–100. Charlottesville, Va., 1991.

Kelso, William. "The Archaeology of Slave Life at Thomas Jefferson's Monticello: 'A Wolf by the Ears.'" *Journal of New World Archaeology* 6, no. 4 (1986): 5–20.

——. *Kingsmill Plantations, 1619–1800: Archaeology of Country Life in Colonial Virginia*. New York, 1984.

King, Julia. "A Comparative Midden Analysis of a Household and Inn in St. Mary's City, Maryland." *Historical Archaeology* 22, no. 2 (1988): 17–39.

——, and Henry Miller. "The View from the Midden: An Analysis of Midden Distribution and Composition at the van Sweringen Site, St. Mary's City, Maryland." *Historical Archaeology* 21, no. 2 (1987): 37–59.

Lounsbury, Carl. *An Illustrated Glossary of Early Southern Architecture and Landscape*. Oxford, 1994.

Malone, Dumas. *Jefferson and His Time*. 6 vols. Boston, 1948.

Marmon, Lee. "Poplar Forest Research Report, Revised Edition." 3 vols. MS on file, Thomas Jefferson's Poplar Forest. Forest, Va., 1991.

Martin, Ann Smart. *Buying into the World of Goods: Eighteenth-Century Consumerism and the Retail Trade from London to the Virginia Frontier*. Ann Arbor, Mich., 1993.

Miller, George L. "Classification and Economic Scaling of 19th Century Ceramics." *Historical Archaeology* 14 (1980): 1–40.

——. "A Revised Set of CC Index Values for Classification and Economic Scaling of English Ceramics from 1787 to 1880." *Historical Archaeology* 25, no. 1 (1991): 1–25.

Moore, Stacy Gibbons. "Established and Well Cultivated, Afro-American Foodways in Early Virginia." *Virginia Cavalcade* 39, no. 2 (1989): 70–83.

Mullin, Michael. *Africa in America: Slave Acculturation and Resistance in the American South and British Caribbean, 1736–1831.* Urbana, Ill., 1992.

Parker, Freddie L. *Stealing a Little Freedom: Advertisements for Slave Runaways in North Carolina, 1791–1840.* New York, 1994.

Perdue, Charles L. Jr., Thomas E. Barden, and Robert K. Phillips, eds. *Weevils in the Wheat: Interviews with Virginia Ex-Slaves.* Charlottesville, Va., 1976.

Pogue, Dennis J., and Esther C. White. "Summary Report on the 'House for Families' Slave Quarter Site (44Fx 762/40–47), Mount Vernon Plantation, Mount Vernon, Virginia." File report no. 2. Mount Vernon, Va., 1991.

Raymer, Leslie. "Macroplant Remains from the Jefferson's Poplar Forest Slave Quarter: A Study in African American Subsistence Practices." New South Associates Technical Report no. 402. Stone Mountain, Ga., 1996.

Samford, Patricia. "The Archaeology of African-American Slavery and Material Culture." *William and Mary Quarterly*, 3d ser., 53, no. 1 (1996): 87–114.

———. "'Strong Is the Bond of Kinship': West African-Style Ancestor Shrines in Sub-floor Pits on African-American Quarters." In *Historical Archaeology and Current Perspectives on Ethnicity*, ed. Maria Franklin and Garrett R. Fesler. Williamsburg, Va. (forthcoming).

Sanford, Douglas. "The Archaeology of Plantation Slavery in Piedmont Virginia: Context and Process." In *Historical Archaeology of the Chesapeake*, ed. Paul A. Shackel and Barbara J. Little, 115–30. Washington, D.C., 1994.

Savitt, Todd L. *Fevers, Agues, and Cures: Medical Life in Old Virginia.* Richmond, 1990.

———. *Medicine and Slavery: The Diseases and Health Care of Blacks in Antebellum Virginia.* Chicago, 1978.

Schlotterbeck, John. "The Internal Economy of Slavery in Rural Piedmont Virginia." *Slavery and Abolition* 12 (1990): 170–81.

Shackel, Paul A., and Barbara J. Little, eds. *Historical Archaeology of the Chesapeake.* Washington, D.C., 1994.

Singleton, Theresa. "The Archaeology of Slave Life." In *Before Freedom Came: African-American Life in the Antebellum South*, ed. Edward D. C. Campbell Jr. with Kym S. Rice, 155–75. Charlottesville, Va., 1991.

Smith, Billy G., and Richard Wojtowicz. *Blacks Who Stole Themselves: Advertisements for Runaways in the* Pennsylvania Gazette, *1728–1790.* Philadelphia, 1989.

Sobel, Mechal. *The World They Made Together: Black and White Values in Eighteenth-Century America.* Princeton, N.J., 1987.

South, Stanley. *Method and Theory in Historical Archaeology.* New York, 1977.

Sprinkle, John H. "The Contents of Charles Cox's Mill House Chest." *Historical Archaeology* 25, no. 3 (1991): 91–93.

Spurrier, John. *The Practical Farmer.* Wilmington, Del., 1793.

St. George, Robert Blair, ed. *Material Life in America.* Boston, 1988.

Stanton, Lucia. *Slavery at Monticello.* Charlottesville, Va., 1996.

Thompson, Mary V. "'They Appear to Live Comfortably Together': Private Life of the Mount Vernon Slaves." MS on file, Mount Vernon Ladies' Association of the Union, Mount Vernon, Va., 1993.

Upton, Dell. "White and Black Landscapes in Eighteenth-Century Virginia." In *Material Life in America*, ed. Robert Blair St. George, 357–70. Boston, 1988.

Vlatch, John Michael. "Plantation Landscapes of

the Antebellum South." In *Before Freedom Came: African-American Life in the Antebellum South*, ed. Edward D. C. Campbell Jr. with Kym S. Rice, 21–47. Charlottesville, Va., 1991.

Windley, Lathan A. *Runaway Slave Advertisements: A Documentary History from the 1730's to 1790.* 4 vols. Westport, Conn., 1983.

Yentsch, Anne. "A Note on a 19th Century Description of Below-Ground 'Storage Cellars' among the Ibo." *African-American Archaeology: Newsletter of the African-American Archaeology Network* 4 (1991): 3–4.

Illustration Credits

Abby Aldrich Rockefeller Folk Art Center, Williamsburg, Va.: fig. 31

Special Collections Library, Duke University, Durham, N.C.: fig. 28

The Huntington Library, San Marino, Calif.: figs. 6, 9

Prints and Photographs Division, Library of Congress, Washington, D.C.: fig. 13

Maryland Historical Society, Baltimore: figs. 24, 30

Massachusetts Historical Society, Boston: figs. 7, 8, 10, 32

Thomas Jefferson's Poplar Forest: figs. 1, 2, 16, 20, 21; photos by Tom Graves, Jr.: 3, 14, 15, 17, 38; photos by Les Schofer: 4, 11, 22, 23, 25, 26, 27, 29, 33, 34, 35, 36, 37; drawing by Hannah Canel: 18; drawing by Rick Potter: 19

Thomas Jefferson Papers, Special Collections Department, University of Virginia Library, Charlottesville: fig. 5

"Tobacco Calendar" was published in Joseph Clarke Robert, *The Tobacco Kingdom: Plantation, Market, and Factory in Virginia and North Carolina, 1800–1860* (Durham, N.C.: Duke University Press, 1938); it first appeared as P. H. Mayo & Brother's "Calendar of Tobacco Cultivation": fig. 12

Index

Hubbard, Jame (headman), 17, 26
Hubbard, Jame, (nailer), 16
Hubbard, Phil, 12, 16, 26, 38, 50, 62

Indian Camp, 11

Jackknives, 48
Jaw bone. *See* Bones
Jefferson, Martha, 9
Jefferson, Thomas, 1, 4, 8, 24, 25, 27, 33, 55, 65, 66; as
    arbiter of disputes, 37, 62; attitude toward doctors,
    18; debt, 10; division of work by gender, 16, 48-49;
    gifts at slave marriages, 13, 55-56; inheritance from
    John Wayles, 9-10; preference for log quarters, 35;
    provisions of food to slaves, 20, 60; purchases from
    slaves, 46, 50; recognition of slave's rights to pri-
    vacy, 38, 64; records of births, 15; sales of slaves,
    12, 13; views of value of slaves' children, 13.
Judith's Creek, 9, 11

Keys, 63

"Lane," *7*, 8
Locks, *5*, 63-64, 65
Lynchburg, 15, 58

Mansion House. *See* Poplar Forest
Marbles, 55
Middens, 33-34, 38, 41, 43, 44, 56
Monticello, 1, 10, 11, 13, 21, 35, 58, 62; Mulberry Row at,
    35; nailery at, 16; spinning at, 16

Nails, 4-5, 35, 41, 42
New London, 15, 51

"Old plantation." *See* Poplar Forest
Orange County, 51
Overseer's house. *See* Poplar Forest

Padlocks. *See* Locks
Pearlware. *See* Ceramics
Peaches, 26. *See also* Plant remains
Pipes (smoking), 19, *20*, 56-58, 65; production of, 56-57.
    See also Tobacco

Plant remains: of food, 58, 59, 60; medicinal, 19; preser-
    vation of, 28
Poplar Forest: blacksmith shop at, 10, 17, 26; dairy at,
    16, 21; early history of, 9; early maps of, 5-8; hospi-
    tal at, 18; Hubbard's house at, *17*; Mansion House
    at, 6; name of, 1; "Old plantation" at, 6; overseer's
    house at, 6; private museum, 4; spinning house at,
    16, 49. *See also* Jefferson, Thomas; Quarter site;
    Slaves
Pots, iron, 3, 55, 58
Prosser, Gabriel, 61

Rakes, 48
Randolph, Martha Jefferson, gift of slaves to, 12
Razor, *41*
Retreat house, *1*, 8. *See also* Poplar Forest
Richmond, 61
Root cellars, *3*, 5, *31*, *34*, 36-37, 38, 40, 56
Ruler, 48, *49*

Scissors, 49, *50*
Seeds. *See* Plant remains
Shadwell, 58
Shears, *50*
Shot, *60*, 61
Slave artisans, 26, 48-49. *See also* Hemmings, John;
    Slaves at Poplar Forest
Slave census, *11*, 13, *14*, *38*
Slave quarters, *2*; abandonment of, 65; archaeological
    excavations at, *3*, 27-46; construction of 33; discov-
    ery of, 3; duplexes as, 38; interpretation of, *66*; lack
    of documentation for, 8; size and location of, 33,
    35, 62; soil chemistry of, 42-43; structural layout of,
    38; —, structure 1, *34*, 35-39, 41, 44, 59; —, struc-
    ture 2, *34*, *35*, 39, 40, 41, 44, 59; —, structure 3, *34*,
    40-41, 45, 46, 59
Slavery: meaning of, 12; resistance to, 13, 48, 63, 66
Slaves, lives of: adornment objects used to express iden-
    tity, *52*, 53, *54*; diet and nutrition, 58-61; earliest
    record at Poplar Forest, 9; family structure, 15;
    health care, 18-19; —, "Negro doctors," 18, *19*,
    70n.16; holidays and leisure activities, 15-16, 53-55;
    literacy, 55; marriage, 13, 15; —, rewards at, 13;
    travel, 16; —, movement between plantations, 11,

15-16, 62; personal choices, 12, 66; privacy, 37-38, 44, 62-64; purchases, 51-53, 63; rations, 60; rebellions, 61; runaways, 12; spiritual beliefs, 18, 37, 56; theft, 12, 37, 48, 63; ways to earn money, 50, 51; work, 2, 13, 15-17, 20-26

Slaves at Poplar Forest: Abby, 16; Aggy, 26, 38; Bess, 16, 26 (*see also* Betty); Betty, 10 (*see also* Bess); Billy Boy, 10 (*see also* Will); Cate, 16, 26; Charles, 10; Davy, 10; Davy (nailer), 16; Dick, 38; Dilcey, 10; Dinah, 11, 38; Doll, 10; Edy, 26; Guinea Will, 10; Hall, 10, 26; Hannah (cook), 55, 71n.10; Hannah (spinner), 38, 62; Hercules, 18; Jerry, 26; John, 10; John (nailer), 16; Lucy, 16; Maria, 12, 16, 26; Mary, 10; Nace (gardener), 12, 26, 37, 62; Nace (headman), 17, 26; Nisy, 16; "Old Judy," 17; Sally, 16; Solomon, 11; Suckey, 10; Will (smith), 17, 26, *52* (*see also* Billy Boy). *See also* Hemmings, John; Hubbard, Jame (headman); Hubbard, Jame (nailer); Hubbard, Phil

Soil chemistry, gardens, 45-46; middens, 43; structure 2, 39; yards, 43-44

Stone ornament, *52*

Straight pins, 49, *50*

Thimbles, 48, 49, *50*

Tobacco, use of: 18-19, 56; cultivation of, 19-24, 26. *See also* Pipes

Tomahawk, 21, 33, 65

Tools, 5, 47-49, 64, 67; used in resistance, 48; storage in root cellar, 37

Trash disposal, 28, 38, 43, 44, 62. *See also* Middens

"Truck patch." *See* Garden

Walnut. *See* Plant remains

War of 1812, 12, 49

Wayles, John, 9-10, 12; estate of, 9; debt of, 10

Wedges, 48, *49*

Wheat, cultivation of, 20, 24-26

Wingos, 10, 11

Writing slate, 55

Yancey, Joel (overseer), 13, *19*

Yards, 33, 43-46, 62, 65